CAMI KOEPP

Dreams of a Forgotten Past

Copyright © 2024 by Cami Koepp

All rights reserved. No part of this publication may be reproduced, stored or transmitted in any form or by any means, electronic, mechanical, photocopying, recording, scanning, or otherwise without written permission from the publisher. It is illegal to copy this book, post it to a website, or distribute it by any other means without permission.

This novel is entirely a work of fiction. The names, characters and incidents portrayed in it are the work of the author's imagination. Any resemblance to actual persons, living or dead, events or localities is entirely coincidental.

Cami Koepp asserts the moral right to be identified as the author of this work.

Cami Koepp has no responsibility for the persistence or accuracy of URLs for external or third-party Internet Websites referred to in this publication and does not guarantee that any content on such Websites is, or will remain, accurate or appropriate.

Designations used by companies to distinguish their products are often claimed as trademarks. All brand names and product names used in this book and on its cover are trade names, service marks, trademarks and registered trademarks of their respective owners. The publishers and the book are not associated with any product or vendor mentioned in this book. None of the companies referenced within the book have endorsed the book.

First edition

This book was professionally typeset on Reedsy.
Find out more at reedsy.com

Contents

1	A Letter from the Abyss	1
2	The Key to the Manor	6
3	A Stranger's Warning	11
4	Shadows of the Manor	17
5	Echoes in the Fog	22
6	The Diary of a Forgotten Soul	27
7	Secrets Beneath the Waves	32
8	Colliding Realities	37
9	Ghosts in the Mirror	43
10	The Forbidden Affair	48
11	Unearthing the Pendant	53
12	The Watcher in the Shadows	58
13	The Secret Room	63
14	The Betrayal	68
15	The Masquerade Ball	73
16	Beneath the Chapel	78
17	The Sinister Gathering	83
18	The Fractured Choice	88
19	The Silent Reckoning	93
20	The Quill and the Key	98
21	Whispers in the Wind	103
22	The First Word	108
23	The Unwritten Page	113
24	The Forgotten Ending	118
25	The Eternal Echo	123

One

A Letter from the Abyss

The rain fell in a relentless torrent, beating against the narrow windows of Elena Moretti's apartment in the heart of Rome. The storm's persistent rhythm played like a symphony of unease, harmonizing with the chaos of her thoughts. She sat at her cluttered desk, her dark hair pulled into a loose bun, stray strands clinging to her damp forehead. Architectural blueprints were scattered in disarray, half-buried beneath old postcards, a chipped mug of espresso, and unopened letters.

She rubbed her temples, her mind fatigued from the monotony of drafting designs that no longer stirred her soul. Her ambition, once fierce and unrelenting, now felt like a shadow of its former self. It wasn't just her career that felt hollow—her entire life seemed to be caught in a liminal space between apathy and yearning.

That's when she noticed it.

The letter. It had been there for weeks, lost amid the mess. The envelope was unlike the others—aged and yellowed, the edges slightly frayed. The handwriting on the front was elegant, slanted with the grace of a bygone era.

To: Giulia Moretti.

Her grandmother.

Elena's heart gave a small jolt. Her grandmother had passed away nearly a decade ago, leaving behind only fragmented stories and an old photograph album she had never gotten around to opening. How had this letter found its way to her?

She turned it over, her fingers tracing the wax seal, imprinted with an insignia she didn't recognize—a crescent moon encircling a single rose. The seal crumbled as she broke it, the faint scent of lavender rising from the parchment.

Inside was a single sheet of paper, its edges curling with time.

Dearest Giulia,
 There is much I regret, but I cannot let this go unsaid. You once told me love was a bridge between two worlds, but now I see it was a tether—binding us in ways I never understood. By the time you read this, the truth will be buried beneath the weight of lies, as will I.
 Montecarvo holds all the answers. The manor is the key. But beware of the shadows—they have teeth, and they remember.
 Alessandro Vitale.

Elena's breath caught. The name was unfamiliar, but there was something about the tone, the desperation in the words, that made her skin prickle. She read the letter again, slower this time, committing each word to memory.

Montecarvo. The manor. Shadows with teeth.

She leaned back, her chair creaking under her weight. Her grandmother had never mentioned Alessandro Vitale, let alone a place called Montecarvo.

Giulia had always been a mystery, her past a series of disjointed anecdotes that hinted at a life far more intriguing than she ever let on.

Elena folded the letter and slipped it back into the envelope, her pulse quickening. She couldn't ignore the strange sense of foreboding the words carried.

But the letter wasn't the only thing in the envelope.

At the bottom was a small, rusted key, intricately carved with a pattern of vines and stars. Its weight was heavier than it looked, as though it carried the burden of countless secrets.

She turned it over in her palm, studying the craftsmanship. The design seemed familiar, but she couldn't place it. And then there was the map. It was crude, sketched on thin paper with ink that had faded to a dull gray, but it clearly marked a path to Montecarvo—a village tucked away in the Italian countryside.

Elena's fingers trembled as she held the map up to the light. She traced the route with her finger, noting the landmarks: a winding river, dense woods, and a lone structure marked as La Villa Oscura—The Dark Manor.

The sound of the rain grew louder, or perhaps it was her pulse pounding in her ears. She felt as though she were standing on the edge of a precipice, staring down into a past she had never been part of yet could almost remember.

Her phone buzzed, snapping her out of her trance. It was her friend Claudia, likely calling to discuss some mundane detail about their weekend plans. Elena silenced it. The world outside her apartment felt inconsequential now, its demands far too ordinary to compete with the enigma in her hands.

What kind of love drove someone to write a letter like this? To speak of shadows and teeth, of buried truths and tethered souls? And why had Alessandro chosen Giulia as the keeper of his secrets?

The key gleamed faintly in the dim light, its purpose both enticing and ominous. She had no answers, only questions that multiplied with every passing second. She felt an unshakable pull toward Montecarvo, as though the very blood in her veins was urging her to go.

Elena's thoughts were interrupted by a sharp knock at her door. She glanced at the clock—it was past midnight. Her neighborhood was quiet, the kind of place where unexpected visitors at such an hour were unheard of.

Her chest tightened as the knock came again, louder this time. She hesitated, her fingers gripping the letter like a lifeline. Slowly, she rose from her chair, her bare feet silent against the cold wooden floor.

She peered through the peephole but saw nothing—only the distorted blur of the hallway light.

"Elena," a voice called softly, almost a whisper. It was muffled but unmistakably male. Her heart froze. No one had announced themselves by name.

She stepped back, clutching the key and letter to her chest. The rain outside seemed to grow fiercer, the wind howling like a warning. Another knock, followed by silence.

When she finally summoned the courage to open the door, the hallway was empty. No sign of anyone. But lying on the floor was a single red rose, its petals glistening with raindrops, and a note tied to its stem.

Montecarvo awaits.

Elena slammed the door shut, her breathing shallow, her mind racing. The key in her hand felt heavier than ever, its cold metal biting into her palm.

Who had sent the letter? Who was watching her? And why did it feel like the shadows were closing in, even here, in the supposed safety of her home?

She had no choice now. Montecarvo held the answers, and she was going to find them—no matter what waited for her in the dark.

Two

The Key to the Manor

Elena stood on the cobblestone street of Montecarvo, clutching her suitcase in one hand and the letter in the other. The village was a strange mix of beauty and desolation, its charm marred by an eerie stillness that seemed to cling to every shadow. The air was thick with the scent of damp earth and pine, mingling with the faint aroma of bread wafting from a nearby bakery. Despite the idyllic surroundings, she couldn't shake the feeling that she was being watched.

The train ride from Rome had been uneventful, though her mind had raced the entire journey, replaying the strange events of the previous night. The rose. The whispered voice. The note urging her to come here. It all felt surreal, like she had stepped into someone else's life. But now that she was here, standing in the very village her grandmother's letter had pointed her to, the surrealism gave way to unease.

Montecarvo was small, its streets winding like veins through clusters of stone buildings with moss-covered roofs. Most windows were shuttered, as though the village itself was hiding from the world. A few locals cast wary glances in her direction, their conversations dropping to hushed murmurs as she passed.

Elena Moretti? a gruff voice called from behind her. She turned to see a wiry man in his sixties, his face lined with age and his expression unreadable. He wore a dark overcoat and a flat cap, his eyes sharp as they appraised her.

Yes, she replied, her voice steady despite the knot in her stomach.

The man nodded and gestured toward a battered car parked at the edge of the square. I'm Pietro. I was told to take you to the manor.

By whom? she asked, gripping the letter tighter.

Pietro's mouth twisted into something that wasn't quite a smile. Let's just say the manor has been expecting you.

She hesitated. Every instinct told her to refuse, to turn back, to leave this village and its secrets behind. But the letter, the key, the pull of something she couldn't name—they had brought her this far. With a reluctant nod, she followed Pietro to the car.

The drive was silent, the atmosphere heavy with tension. The road snaked through dense woods, the trees pressing in like a living wall. Pietro's hands gripped the steering wheel tightly, his gaze fixed on the road as though he dared not look at her.

Do you know much about the manor? Elena ventured, breaking the silence.

It's not my place to say, Pietro replied curtly. You'll find out soon enough.

She wanted to press him, to demand answers, but something in his tone warned her against it. Instead, she turned her attention to the scenery, though the towering trees offered little comfort. The further they drove, the darker the forest seemed to grow, as if the sunlight itself was reluctant to enter this place.

Finally, the car emerged into a clearing, and there it stood: La Villa Oscura.

The manor was a hulking structure of weathered stone, its façade overgrown with ivy. Its tall windows were dark, their glass reflecting the gray sky. A wrought-iron gate stood open, its intricate design marred by rust. The sight of it sent a chill down Elena's spine. She had seen the place before—in her dreams.

Pietro cut the engine and turned to her, his expression grave. I'll wait here. If you're not back in an hour, I'll come looking.

Why wouldn't I come back? she asked, her voice sharper than she intended.

He didn't answer, only gestured toward the manor. The key, he said simply.

Elena retrieved the rusted key from her coat pocket and stepped out of the car. The ground beneath her boots was soft with moss, and the air felt colder here, heavier. She approached the front door, her pulse quickening with each step.

The key slid into the lock with surprising ease. As she turned it, the door creaked open, revealing a dimly lit foyer. The air inside was thick with the scent of decay and something else—something faintly sweet, like old roses.

She stepped inside, the sound of her footsteps swallowed by the vast silence. The walls were lined with faded tapestries, their colors dulled by time. A grand staircase curved upward, its wooden banister worn smooth. Everything about the place felt abandoned, yet it carried an inexplicable energy, as though it were waiting for her.

Elena moved cautiously, her eyes scanning every detail. She felt like an intruder, yet something about the manor felt intimately familiar. She followed the hallway to a large drawing room, where a single piece of furniture remained—a piano, its once-polished surface now coated in dust. On the piano's lid lay a book, its cover cracked and worn.

She hesitated before opening it. The pages were filled with handwritten music, the notes flowing like a river of ink. At the bottom of the last page was a signature: *Alessandro Vitale.*

Her fingers trembled as she traced the name. She had found his music, his voice preserved in melody. But why was it still here? Who had left it? And what had happened to him?

A sudden creak behind her shattered her thoughts. She spun around, her heart pounding. The hallway was empty, but the air felt charged, as though someone—or something—was there.

Who's there? she called, her voice echoing through the empty space.

Silence. Then, a faint sound—a whisper, so soft she almost didn't hear it. It came from upstairs.

Clutching the letter and the book, Elena moved toward the staircase. Each step groaned under her weight, the sound like a warning in the stillness. As she reached the landing, she saw it—a door at the end of the hallway, slightly ajar. Light flickered from within, casting shadows that danced along the walls.

Her breath caught as she approached. The whispering grew louder, words she couldn't quite make out. She pushed the door open, her pulse racing.

Inside was a small study, its walls lined with bookshelves. In the center of the room stood a single chair, facing away from her. And in that chair sat a figure, its back to her.

Hello? she said, her voice trembling.

The figure didn't move. She took a cautious step forward, her eyes fixed on the chair. As she reached out to touch it, the figure suddenly slumped forward, revealing an old skeleton dressed in tattered clothing. Clutched in its bony fingers was another letter.

Elena's scream caught in her throat as the candlelight flickered, and the shadows seemed to shift around her. The words etched into the envelope froze her in place:

For Elena Moretti.

The room plunged into darkness.

Three

A Stranger's Warning

The skeleton's hand was still stretched outward, the brittle fingers gripping the letter as if guarding it even in death. Elena's chest tightened. Her feet refused to move, frozen by the surreal horror of the moment. The flickering candlelight seemed to animate the scene, casting grotesque shadows across the room. Every instinct screamed at her to run, but the pull of the envelope—the very fact that it bore her name—anchored her in place.

The air grew colder, pressing against her skin. A distant sound echoed through the manor, a faint creak that could have been the wind but felt more deliberate, more purposeful. Forcing herself to move, Elena stretched out a trembling hand and grasped the envelope. The moment her fingers brushed against it, the skeleton's hand fell apart, crumbling into a pile of dust and bone fragments on the floor.

She stifled a cry, clutching the envelope to her chest. The edges of the paper were yellowed and frayed, but the ink of her name was bold and fresh, as if written just days ago. Who could have known she would come here? And why had this been left in such a chilling manner?

The whispering started again.

It was faint at first, barely audible over her own racing heartbeat. But it grew louder, surrounding her, though she couldn't pinpoint its source. The words were indistinct, a haunting murmuring that filled the air like smoke. Elena spun around, her eyes darting to every corner of the room. The flickering light from the lone candle amplified the eerie movement of the shadows.

Who's there? she called out, her voice unsteady.

No response. The whispering ceased as suddenly as it began, leaving an oppressive silence in its wake.

Elena's breath came in shallow gasps as she turned her attention back to the envelope in her hands. She hesitated for a moment, her thumb running over the wax seal that bore the same crescent moon and rose emblem she had seen before. The familiar symbol filled her with equal parts dread and fascination. She tore the envelope open carefully and unfolded the letter inside.

The handwriting was elegant, sweeping across the page in looping curves:

Elena,
   If you have found this, then you are in grave danger. The truth of Montecarvo is buried beneath layers of deceit, but the past is alive within these walls, watching, waiting. The key you hold is more than it seems—it opens not just doors but paths. Be wary of whom you trust. The shadows have long memories, and the manor has its own way of keeping secrets.

Alessandro Vitale.

Her heart pounded at the sight of the name, the same as the one in the letter to her grandmother. But this wasn't a relic of the past—it had to have been written recently. Yet how could that be possible when Alessandro had vanished decades ago?

Before she could process the implications, the candle abruptly snuffed out, plunging the room into complete darkness.

Elena, a voice whispered, so close it seemed to brush against her ear. She whirled around, clutching the letter, her pulse racing.

Who's there? she demanded, her voice breaking.

Silence. The air grew colder, and her breath became visible in the frigid gloom.

She fumbled for her phone, the only source of light she had. The screen illuminated her shaking hands as she activated the flashlight and swung it around the room. The skeletal remains were still there, motionless and indifferent to the terror unraveling around her. But something was different. The door, which she was certain she had left ajar, was now closed.

Her breathing quickened. Someone—or something—was toying with her.

Gripping the phone like a lifeline, she hurried to the door, her footsteps echoing on the wooden floor. Her fingers wrapped around the cold brass handle, but as she turned it, the door wouldn't budge. She yanked harder, but it was locked from the outside.

Elena, the voice came again, softer this time, almost coaxing. It seemed to emanate from everywhere and nowhere.

No, she muttered, backing away from the door. This isn't real. It can't be real.

But the sensation of being watched was undeniable. She could feel it, the weight of unseen eyes bearing down on her. The flashlight beam trembled as she swung it toward the far corner of the room—and froze.

A figure stood there, barely visible, shrouded in the shadows. It didn't move, didn't speak, but its presence was palpable, an oppressive force that sent a shiver down her spine.

Who are you? Elena demanded, her voice trembling. What do you want?

The figure tilted its head ever so slightly, as if considering her question. Then, without warning, it stepped forward, emerging into the beam of her flashlight.

It was a man, his features sharp and angular, his dark eyes piercing as they locked onto hers. He was dressed in a suit that seemed out of place, its style belonging to a different era. But what struck her most was the unmistakable resemblance to the man in the painting she had seen in the manor earlier.

Elena Moretti, he said, his voice low and melodic. It wasn't a question.

How do you know my name? she demanded, taking a step back.

He didn't answer. Instead, he extended a hand toward her, palm up. You shouldn't be here. The past isn't yours to claim.

Her grip on the letter tightened. What does that mean? Who are you?

You must leave, he said, his tone firm yet strangely gentle. Before it's too late.

I'm not leaving until I get answers, she shot back, her fear giving way to defiance. Who are you? And what happened to Alessandro Vitale?

At the mention of the name, a flicker of something crossed his face—pain, perhaps, or regret. But it was gone as quickly as it appeared.

You're asking the wrong questions, he said. The right ones could cost you everything.

Before she could respond, the man stepped back into the shadows, his form dissolving into the darkness like smoke. The room grew eerily silent once more, the oppressive cold lifting as if whatever presence had been there was now gone.

Elena turned back to the door and tried the handle again. This time, it opened effortlessly. She stumbled into the hallway, her flashlight cutting through the gloom as she tried to steady her breathing.

Pietro was waiting. He had promised to come looking if she didn't return within an hour. But as she descended the grand staircase, she found the foyer empty.

Pietro? she called, her voice echoing through the manor. No answer.

The sound of tires crunching on gravel drew her to the front door. She burst outside just in time to see the taillights of Pietro's car disappearing down the winding road, leaving her stranded.

A chill ran down her spine as she turned back toward the manor. The shadows seemed deeper now, more menacing, as if the house itself were watching her.

In the distance, a single bell tolled, its mournful chime reverberating through the night.

And then she heard it again.

Elena.

The whisper came from behind her, but when she spun around, there was no one there. Only the sprawling forest, dark and endless.

She clutched the letter to her chest, her resolve hardening despite the fear clawing at her. Montecarvo held answers, and she was determined to find them—no matter what waited for her in the shadows.

The bell tolled again, louder this time, as if summoning her deeper into the mystery.

Four

Shadows of the Manor

Elena stood motionless in the manor's crumbling foyer, her breath caught between fear and defiance. The bell that had tolled moments ago still echoed faintly in her ears, each vibration feeling like a call—a command—she couldn't ignore. The shadows that clung to the high ceilings and dusty corners seemed alive, shifting as though they held secrets waiting to be uncovered.

The envelope in her hand trembled. Alessandro Vitale. His name had haunted her grandmother's letter, then again in the skeleton's cryptic warning. Now, it whispered to her through the darkness, calling her deeper into the enigma of Montecarvo.

And Pietro… Pietro was gone. His sudden departure without explanation felt deliberate, almost orchestrated. She pressed her hand against the cold wooden door, debating whether to chase after him, but something held her back.

The manor didn't want her to leave.

A chill brushed her neck, a sensation so vivid that she turned sharply, expecting to find someone standing there. But the hallway was empty. The air had grown thick, dense with an otherworldly weight that pressed against her chest. Her flashlight cut through the gloom, landing on a grand staircase spiraling upward.

Elena...

The whisper came again, this time from above. The voice was faint yet distinct, as though someone stood just out of sight, urging her to follow.

Her fingers tightened around the flashlight as she took her first step onto the staircase. Each creak beneath her weight echoed like a warning. The beam of light danced over the intricate carvings on the banister—twisting vines, crescent moons, and roses intertwined. The design mirrored the emblem on the letter's seal.

Halfway up the staircase, she noticed faint footprints in the thick layer of dust. They weren't hers. Her stomach churned at the realization that someone—or something—had been here recently. The prints led upward, disappearing into the shadows of the second floor.

Who's there? she called, her voice breaking the oppressive silence. The only response was the faint rustling of fabric, like the swish of a long coat brushing against the floor.

Summoning her courage, she reached the top of the stairs. The hallway stretched before her, lined with closed doors, their brass handles dulled with age. One door at the end stood slightly ajar, light spilling through the crack like a beacon.

Elena's steps were slow and deliberate as she approached, her pulse quickening with each step. She pushed the door open fully, revealing a grand library. Dust motes floated in the dim light of a single oil lamp on a desk in the center of the room. The shelves were lined with books, their spines cracked and faded, their titles obscured by time.

But it wasn't the books that caught her attention. It was the figure seated at the desk, his back to her.

Her breath caught in her throat. The man was writing furiously, his hand gliding across the page as though time itself depended on his haste. His dark hair was slightly disheveled, and his shoulders were tense with purpose.

Elena Moretti, he said without turning around, his voice smooth yet tinged with something indefinable—sorrow, perhaps, or regret.

How do you know my name? she demanded, her voice steadier than she felt.

The man paused, setting the pen down with deliberate care. He didn't answer immediately. Instead, he reached for a book on the desk and opened it to a marked page.

You've come far, haven't you? he said, his tone soft but weighted. But every step you take pulls you closer to the truth—and to danger.

She took a cautious step forward. Who are you? Are you… Alessandro Vitale?

The man stiffened, his hand gripping the edge of the desk. That name… It carries more than you realize.

He rose from the chair slowly, turning to face her. Elena's flashlight illuminated his face—a face that felt achingly familiar. His dark eyes were sharp, and his features were striking, as though carved from marble. But there was a heaviness in his expression, a weariness that spoke of lifetimes lived.

Some truths are better left buried, he said, his gaze locking onto hers.

I didn't come here for riddles, she shot back, her frustration overpowering her fear. I want answers. Why did you write to my grandmother? What happened to you? To her?

The man stepped closer, his presence commanding yet oddly comforting. You think you're here by chance? That this is just a mystery to solve? This manor has a will of its own, Elena. It chose you.

Her pulse quickened. Chose me for what?

To finish what your grandmother started, he said simply.

Before she could respond, the oil lamp flickered violently, casting the room into momentary darkness. A sudden gust of wind tore through the library, toppling books and extinguishing the flame entirely.

Elena, leave now, the man said urgently, his voice cutting through the chaos.

What's happening? she shouted, panic rising.

They know you're here, he said, his face illuminated briefly by the beam of her flashlight. The shadows—they won't let you go so easily.

As if on cue, the room grew impossibly cold. The shelves groaned, and the walls seemed to close in. The shadows that danced along the edges of her flashlight's beam grew darker, more solid. They began to move, slithering toward her like living things.

Elena! the man shouted. He grabbed her arm and pulled her toward the door. Run!

She stumbled into the hallway, her flashlight barely cutting through the oppressive darkness. The man stayed close behind her, his grip firm as he guided her toward the staircase.

They'll try to stop you, he said. Don't look back, no matter what you hear.

What are they? she asked, her voice trembling.

Remnants of the past, he replied. Memories that refuse to die.

As they reached the top of the staircase, the shadows surged forward, their forms taking shape—faces, arms, and voices that cried out in anguish.

Elena…

The whisper was louder now, almost a roar. It came from everywhere, reverberating through her very bones.

She turned her head instinctively, unable to resist the pull. Her flashlight caught a fleeting glimpse of a woman's face in the shadows—a face that looked like her own.

Elena, don't! the man shouted, pulling her forward.

But it was too late. The image burned into her mind, a haunting reflection of herself, and her foot slipped on the top step. She fell forward, the world spinning as the shadows swallowed her scream.

Five

Echoes in the Fog

Pain. It was the first thing Elena registered as she awoke, sprawled at the bottom of the staircase. Her head throbbed, her ankle ached, and her palms stung from the impact. For a moment, she stayed still, her breath shallow as she tried to piece together what had happened.

The shadows. The face. The man.

Elena, his voice cut through the fog of her mind, firm yet frantic.

She turned her head to see him kneeling beside her. His face was pale, his dark eyes scanning her for injuries. You fell, he said. You're lucky it wasn't worse.

Her voice came out hoarse. What… what were those things?

He hesitated, as though weighing how much to tell her. They're remnants of what the manor holds—memories made manifest. They're not alive, but they're not dead either. They're something in between.

The explanation made no sense, but her mind was too muddled to challenge it. She tried to sit up, but pain shot through her ankle, forcing a gasp from her lips.

You've twisted it, he said, his tone softening. You can't walk like this.

I don't have a choice, she replied through gritted teeth. I need answers, and I'm not leaving without them.

A flicker of admiration crossed his face, but it was quickly replaced by concern. Answers won't matter if you don't make it out alive.

Then help me, she demanded. You seem to know more about this place than anyone. Who are you? Why are you here?

He stood and paced a few steps away, his figure half-obscured by the dim light of her fallen flashlight. I told you before: I am a part of this story. Just as you are.

That's not an answer, she shot back. What are you hiding?

His shoulders tensed, and for a long moment, he didn't respond. When he finally spoke, his voice was barely audible. I've been here longer than you can imagine, tied to this place in ways I can't fully explain. What I do know is that your arrival has set things in motion that cannot be undone.

Elena's chest tightened. The cryptic warnings, the shadows, the strange familiarity of the manor—it all pointed to a truth she wasn't sure she was ready to face. Are you Alessandro Vitale? she asked again, her voice trembling.

His gaze locked onto hers, unflinching. I was.

The room seemed to grow colder at his admission, the weight of his words pressing down on her like a physical force. You're... a ghost?

Not exactly, he said, his expression unreadable. I'm something left behind—a fragment of what I once was.

The surreal nature of the conversation threatened to overwhelm her, but she forced herself to focus. Why me? Why did you write to my grandmother? What does this have to do with her?

Giulia and I... His voice faltered, and for the first time, she saw a crack in his composure. We loved each other, but our love came at a cost. The manor... it doesn't let go of those who betray it.

Betray it? Elena echoed.

Before he could answer, the shadows began to stir again, coiling at the edges of the room like a living mist. Alessandro's expression hardened. We don't have much time. They'll come back stronger.

She gritted her teeth and tried to stand, wincing as pain shot through her ankle. Alessandro moved to her side, his arm steadying her. Lean on me, he said.

With his help, she managed to hobble toward the library, the room's heavy oak doors offering a semblance of protection. As they crossed the threshold, Alessandro shut the doors behind them and dragged a nearby bookshelf in front of them, barricading the entrance.

The library was dimly lit by the moonlight streaming through a crack in the curtains. The air felt marginally safer here, though the ever-present tension remained.

Giulia left me a letter, Elena said, breaking the silence. She was connected to this place. To you. What happened to her?

Alessandro's jaw tightened, and he turned away, his hands braced against the desk. She tried to save me. But the manor demanded its due. It always does.

The weight of his words sent a shiver down her spine. What do you mean?

He faced her, his expression grave. This place... it feeds on the pain of those who enter. Betrayal, loss, love—it consumes them, weaving them into the fabric of the manor. Giulia paid the price for loving me, just as you're at risk now.

Elena's throat tightened. Why? Why would the manor care about any of this?

The manor is more than just a house, he said. It's alive in its own way, a vessel for memories too powerful to fade. It keeps them, nurtures them, and punishes those who disturb its balance.

The shadows outside the library door began to thrum against the wood, their whispers growing louder and more insistent.

You can still leave, Alessandro said urgently. The manor hasn't claimed you fully yet. If you go now, you might escape.

She met his gaze, her resolve hardening. I'm not leaving. Not until I understand why this is happening. Not until I know the truth about my grandmother.

His expression was a mixture of admiration and despair. Then you need to find the chapel, he said. It's the only place where the manor's influence weakens. The answers you seek might be there.

Before she could ask him how to find it, the shadows surged against the door with a deafening crash. The barricade trembled, the bookshelf sliding slightly under the pressure.

They're here, Alessandro said, his voice taut with urgency. We have to move.

Elena grabbed her flashlight and limped toward the far side of the library, where Alessandro pointed to a hidden panel in the wall. He pushed it open, revealing a narrow passageway that descended into darkness.

This leads to the chapel, he said. But the path won't be easy.

What about you? she asked, her voice trembling.

I'll hold them off, he said. Go, Elena. Now!

Before she could argue, the door burst open, and the shadows poured into the room, their forms writhing and twisting. Alessandro stepped forward, his figure glowing faintly as he faced them.

Elena, go! he shouted, his voice echoing with a power that made her chest ache.

She hesitated for a heartbeat, then plunged into the passageway, the door slamming shut behind her. Darkness enveloped her, and the last thing she heard was Alessandro's voice, fading into the cacophony of the shadows:

Find the truth… before it's too late.

Six

The Diary of a Forgotten Soul

Elena stumbled down the narrow passageway, her hands outstretched to steady herself against the damp stone walls. The darkness was oppressive, swallowing the beam of her flashlight, leaving her with only a few feet of visibility. Her breath came in shallow gasps, the adrenaline from her escape still coursing through her veins.

The sound of Alessandro's voice, shouting in defiance against the shadows, echoed in her mind, accompanied by the cacophony of inhuman whispers that had filled the library. Guilt clawed at her—she had left him behind to face them alone. But what choice had she had? He had insisted, practically pushed her into the passageway. Now, she was alone, with no idea what lay ahead.

The passage twisted and turned, descending deeper into the earth. The air grew colder, the scent of damp stone and earth mingling with something faintly metallic. Her flashlight flickered, sending a spike of panic through her. She slapped it against her palm until the beam steadied, though it felt as if the darkness pressed closer with every step.

Ahead, the passage widened, revealing a small chamber. Elena paused, her flashlight sweeping across the space. It was empty except for a wooden table in the center, its surface littered with papers and a single oil lamp that seemed impossibly out of place. The lamp was unlit, yet it gleamed as if polished recently.

Her heartbeat quickened. Someone had been here. Recently.

She approached the table cautiously, her eyes scanning the papers. Most were yellowed and torn, filled with indecipherable scribbles, but one stood out—a leather-bound diary, its cover embossed with a delicate rose-and-crescent-moon design. The sight of the emblem sent a shiver through her.

Elena hesitated before opening it, the leather soft and worn beneath her fingertips. The first page bore a name written in elegant script: Giulia Moretti.

Her breath hitched. This was her grandmother's.

She flipped to the first entry, her fingers trembling. The date at the top was nearly seventy years old, written long before Giulia had become the quiet, enigmatic woman Elena had known.

April 4th, 1954: Today, I met Alessandro Vitale.

Elena's heart raced as she read on.

He is not like the others in Montecarvo. There is a fire in his eyes, a defiance that mirrors my own. I should not feel drawn to him—it is dangerous for us both. But his smile, his voice... they are impossible to ignore. He speaks of freedom, of breaking the chains that bind this village to its dark history. I want to believe him. I want to help him. But I fear what may come of it.

Elena turned the page, desperate for more. The entries painted a picture of a love that grew in secret, shared in stolen moments beneath the shadow of the manor. But there was also fear—Giulia wrote of Alessandro's determination to challenge the powerful families who ruled Montecarvo, families who guarded the manor's secrets with ruthless precision.

One entry stopped Elena cold.

June 19th, 1954: Alessandro believes the manor itself is alive, that it feeds on the pain and betrayal of those who dwell within its walls. He says it has eyes that see beyond time, ears that hear the whispers of the heart. I laughed at him, but now... I am not so sure. I feel its presence, always watching, waiting. We must leave this place, or it will destroy us both.

Elena's flashlight flickered again, pulling her back to the present. The chamber felt colder, the air heavier. She could almost feel the weight of her grandmother's fear, the urgency that bled through her words.

She turned another page, her heart aching as she read Giulia's final entry.

July 8th, 1954: Alessandro is gone. They came for him in the night, their footsteps silent but their intent clear. I hid as he instructed, but I heard everything—the struggle, his cries. I wanted to scream, to fight, but I could not move. I am a coward, and now he is lost. I can feel the manor's triumph, its hunger sated. I must leave Montecarvo, but part of me will always remain here, bound to him. To this place.

Elena stared at the words, her vision blurring with unshed tears. Her grandmother had been here, had loved and lost Alessandro within these very walls. The guilt and pain Giulia must have carried for the rest of her life felt unbearable.

A sudden sound jolted her—a faint rustling, like fabric brushing against stone. She spun around, the flashlight trembling in her hand. The passage was empty, but the sound came again, closer this time.

Elena... The whisper was soft, almost tender, but it carried a weight that sent chills down her spine.

She backed away from the passage, her flashlight beam darting across the chamber. Her hand brushed against the oil lamp, and without thinking, she lit it with the lighter she carried. The warm glow filled the space, but it did little to chase away the feeling of being watched.

Elena... The voice came again, louder now. It was unmistakably Alessandro's, but it was different—hollow, as though carried on the wind.

Alessandro? she called, her voice shaking.

The rustling grew louder, and from the shadows of the passage emerged a figure. It was Alessandro, but something was wrong. His features were sharper, his eyes darker, and his movements were unnervingly smooth, almost gliding.

You shouldn't have come here, he said, his voice echoing unnaturally.

Alessandro? she whispered again, her knees threatening to buckle under the weight of her fear.

He stepped closer, his form wavering like a reflection in rippling water. The manor doesn't forgive, he said, his voice layered with an otherworldly timbre. It will take what it is owed.

What does that mean? she demanded, backing against the table.

Before he could answer, the oil lamp flickered violently, and the chamber was plunged into darkness. Elena's flashlight died completely, leaving her in suffocating blackness. The sound of Alessandro's voice mixed with the whispers of the shadows, growing louder, closer.

Elena... run.

And then the chamber erupted with a deafening roar as the walls themselves seemed to come alive, the shadows surging toward her with terrifying speed.

Seven

Secrets Beneath the Waves

Elena's scream was swallowed by the darkness as the shadows surged around her, their cold, twisting forms brushing against her skin. The roar of the walls felt like they were collapsing in on themselves, an echoing cacophony that rattled her bones. She stumbled backward, clutching the diary against her chest as though it could protect her.

Elena, move! Alessandro's voice rang out, commanding and sharp, yet she couldn't see him.

Where? she shouted, her voice trembling.

Follow the light! he barked.

Light? There was none. The oil lamp had gone out, and her flashlight was useless. Her pulse thundered in her ears, and for a brief, paralyzing moment, she thought this was where it would end—in the clutches of shadows that fed on pain and betrayal.

And then she saw it—a faint glimmer, like moonlight reflecting on water, just beyond the edges of the chamber. It was subtle, almost imperceptible, but it was there. With a surge of desperate hope, she stumbled toward it, ignoring the sharp, icy fingers of the shadows tugging at her coat and hair.

The light grew brighter as she moved, revealing a narrow tunnel leading away from the chamber. The walls glistened with moisture, and the air smelled of salt and decay. She didn't question it. Survival was all that mattered.

Elena, don't stop! Alessandro's voice urged her, though it was growing fainter, as though he were being pulled in the opposite direction.

I can't see you! she cried.

You're not supposed to, he said cryptically. Go!

The tunnel sloped downward, the floor slick beneath her boots. She clung to the walls for balance, her fingers grazing the wet stone. The shadows were close behind her now, their whispers becoming guttural snarls. The air was growing colder, biting at her exposed skin, and she felt as though the walls were pressing closer with each step.

Just when she thought she couldn't go any further, the tunnel opened into a vast underground cavern. The ceiling was high, its jagged edges dripping with stalactites that sparkled faintly in the strange, ethereal light that filled the space. At the center of the cavern was a pool of water, its surface unnaturally still and glowing with an otherworldly blue hue.

Elena stumbled to the edge of the pool, her breaths ragged. The shadows hesitated at the entrance of the cavern, writhing as if repelled by the light. But she could feel their malevolence, their hunger. They wouldn't stay back forever.

Elena...

The voice came again, softer now, almost gentle. But it wasn't Alessandro's this time. It was a woman's, and it sent a shiver down her spine.

She turned toward the pool, her heart pounding. The glowing water began to ripple, though there was no breeze, no disturbance. Slowly, a figure emerged from the depths—a woman with pale skin, dark hair flowing like ink around her, and eyes that bore an uncanny resemblance to Elena's own.

Who are you? Elena whispered, her voice trembling.

The woman tilted her head, a sad smile playing on her lips. You know me, she said, her voice echoing softly in the cavern.

No... I don't, Elena said, though even as the words left her lips, she felt the lie in them. There was something achingly familiar about the woman, something that tugged at the deepest recesses of her memory.

You carry my blood, the woman said, her tone gentle but firm. And my burden.

Realization washed over Elena like a wave. Giulia, she breathed.

Her grandmother—no, not her grandmother as she had known her, but a younger version, preserved in a moment of time that felt both impossibly distant and disturbingly close.

You've come further than I dared, Giulia said, stepping onto the edge of the pool, though her feet left no marks on the damp ground. But you're not safe here. The manor will not let you leave without its due.

I don't understand, Elena said, clutching the diary tighter. Why did you write this? Why did you send me here?

Giulia's expression darkened, her sadness deepening. I didn't send you. The manor did. It knew you would come, just as it knew I would fail.

Fail at what? Elena demanded, her frustration bubbling to the surface. Why is this happening? Why me?

Because you are the only one left who can end this, Giulia said. The manor feeds on pain, on betrayal, on the love we couldn't protect. Alessandro and I... we thought we could escape, but we were wrong. The manor took him, and it will take you too if you let it.

Tears stung Elena's eyes. He's still here, she said. I've seen him. I've spoken to him.

Giulia shook her head. What you've seen is only a fragment, a shadow of who he was. The real Alessandro is gone, consumed by the manor. And soon, you will be too if you stay.

No, Elena said fiercely. There has to be a way to stop it. To free him. To free you.

Giulia hesitated, her gaze shifting to the pool. There is one way, she said. But it requires a sacrifice greater than you can imagine.

What kind of sacrifice? Elena asked, her voice barely above a whisper.

Before Giulia could answer, the shadows surged into the cavern, their hesitation replaced by a newfound fury. The light from the pool flickered as the darkness closed in, and Elena felt the cold, clawing tendrils brush against her once more.

Run, Elena! Giulia cried, her voice echoing with urgency.

But there was nowhere to run. The shadows were everywhere now, circling the pool, cutting off her escape. The water began to churn violently, and the glowing light dimmed, leaving Elena in near-complete darkness.

Elena! Alessandro's voice rang out from the shadows, distant yet desperate.

Alessandro! she screamed, spinning in place, her flashlight useless against the encroaching darkness.

The shadows lunged, and the last thing Elena saw was Giulia's face, her expression a mix of sorrow and resolve, as the cavern was swallowed by the abyss.

Eight

Colliding Realities

Elena gasped as the shadows enveloped her, a suffocating chill sinking into her bones. She couldn't see, couldn't move, couldn't breathe. It felt as though the darkness was alive, prying at the edges of her mind, whispering her worst fears and regrets back to her. Her legs buckled, and she collapsed to her knees, the diary slipping from her grasp and hitting the cavern floor with a dull thud.

Elena, the voice of Alessandro broke through the chaos, faint but insistent, a thread of hope in the suffocating abyss. You have to fight it!

Fight it? How could she fight something that wasn't tangible, that existed only as an endless, formless void? The whispers grew louder, overlapping now, distinct words slipping through the cacophony.

You failed her… Just like Giulia… You'll never escape…

No! she screamed, her voice ragged.

But the shadows pressed harder, winding tighter around her body, seeping into her skin. Memories she didn't recognize—of betrayal, anguish, and loss—flashed in her mind, and she couldn't tell if they were hers or someone else's.

Through the chaos, she felt a sudden warmth, faint but unmistakable, like sunlight breaking through heavy clouds. She clung to it, focusing on the sensation, willing it to grow stronger. Slowly, the oppressive cold began to recede, the whispers dimming into background noise.

Elena! Alessandro's voice was louder now, closer.

She opened her eyes to find herself lying on the cavern floor, the glowing pool of water now calm and still beside her. Alessandro knelt at her side, his hands gripping her shoulders, his dark eyes filled with concern.

What happened? she asked, her voice trembling.

The shadows tried to consume you, he said, his voice taut with urgency. But you resisted. That's the only reason you're still here.

She sat up slowly, her entire body trembling. The cavern was silent again, though the air still felt heavy, charged with an unseen energy. The diary lay nearby, its pages fanned open as if waiting for her to pick it up again.

Giulia was gone.

Where is she? Elena asked, turning to Alessandro. Giulia—she was here.

She came to warn you, he said, his expression grim. But the manor doesn't allow those it claims to linger for long. She's part of this place now, just like I am.

Elena's throat tightened. She said there was a way to stop this. To end it.

Alessandro's face darkened. If there is, it comes at a cost.

What cost? she pressed.

Before he could answer, a tremor rippled through the cavern, the ground shifting beneath them. The glowing pool began to churn once more, the light dimming as cracks spidered across the walls.

We have to move, Alessandro said, pulling her to her feet.

They stumbled back toward the tunnel, but as they reached the entrance, the air shimmered like heat rising from pavement. A moment later, they were no longer in the cavern.

Instead, they stood in the grand foyer of the manor, its once-empty space now filled with ghostly figures. Men and women in clothing from different eras milled about as if attending a party, their movements fluid yet disconnected, their faces blurred and indistinct.

What is this? Elena whispered, her heart pounding.

The manor's memories, Alessandro said. You're seeing fragments of what it's taken.

One of the figures turned toward her, its blurred face contorting into something almost human. Elena, it rasped, the sound grating and hollow.

She stumbled back, clutching Alessandro's arm. Why do they keep calling my name?

Because you're the last piece, he said, his tone heavy with meaning. The manor needs you to complete its story. To finish what started decades ago.

The figures began to move closer, their blurred features sharpening into hollow eyes and skeletal grins. One reached for her, its hand passing through Alessandro as though he weren't there.

You can't stay here, he said urgently, pulling her toward the staircase.

Where can I go? she asked, panic rising.

The chapel, he said. If you can make it there, you might have a chance.

They climbed the stairs, the ghostly figures following, their movements growing more frantic. The whispers began again, weaving around her like a poisonous fog.

You can't escape... You'll betray him, just like she did...

She shook her head, trying to block out the voices. They're lying, she said aloud, though part of her wasn't sure.

They're not lying, Alessandro said, his voice bitter. The manor doesn't lie. It shows the truth in the cruelest way possible.

They reached the top of the staircase, and Alessandro led her down a hallway that seemed to stretch endlessly. Doors lined the walls, some ajar to reveal glimpses of impossible scenes: a ballroom filled with dancing couples; a war-torn battlefield; a woman crying over a child's lifeless body.

This isn't real, Elena said, her voice trembling.

It's real enough, Alessandro replied. Keep moving.

At the end of the hallway was a door unlike the others, its surface carved with the same rose-and-crescent-moon emblem she had seen before. Alessandro pushed it open, revealing a spiral staircase that descended into darkness.

This leads to the chapel, he said.

Elena hesitated, her gaze flicking back to the figures closing in on them. What about you?

I'll hold them off, he said.

No! she said, grabbing his arm. I'm not leaving you behind.

You don't have a choice, he said, his expression pained. If you don't go now, everything we've done will be for nothing.

The ghostly figures were almost upon them, their skeletal hands reaching for her. Alessandro turned to face them, his form glowing faintly.

Go, Elena! he shouted.

She hesitated for one agonizing moment, then plunged into the darkness of the staircase. As she descended, the whispers grew louder, merging into a deafening roar that seemed to come from within her own mind.

At the bottom of the staircase was another door, its surface scarred and weathered. She pushed it open, and her breath caught in her throat.

The chapel was nothing like she had expected. It was small and unadorned, the stone walls bare except for a single altar at the center. On the altar lay a book, its cover identical to Giulia's diary, but this one pulsed with an eerie light.

Elena stepped forward, her hand reaching for the book. But before she could touch it, the door slammed shut behind her, and a voice echoed through the chapel.

You've come far, Elena, it said, deep and resonant. But are you prepared to pay the price?

She turned to face the source of the voice—and froze.

Standing before her was Giulia, but her face was twisted into something unrecognizable, her eyes burning with an unnatural light.

Elena, she said, her voice both familiar and alien. It's time to choose.

Nine

Ghosts in the Mirror

Elena's breath hitched as she stared at the figure standing before her. It was her grandmother—or, at least, something that resembled her. The woman's features were twisted, her once-gentle eyes now glowing with an unnatural light, and her voice carried an unsettling resonance.

Giulia? Elena whispered, her voice trembling.

The figure tilted its head, a crooked smile spreading across her lips. I was Giulia once. Now, I am what remains—a fragment bound to this place, just as Alessandro is. And now, Elena… so are you.

No, Elena said, her voice growing stronger. I don't belong to this place. I came here for answers, and I won't leave without them.

Giulia—or the entity wearing her face—stepped closer, her presence sending a chill through the air. The answers you seek have a price, Elena. Are you willing to pay it?

Elena clenched her fists, her gaze darting to the glowing book on the altar.

It pulsed faintly, as if alive, drawing her closer even as dread coiled in her stomach. What's in the book? she asked.

Your truth, the figure replied. The truth of what binds you to this place. To us.

Why do I need to be bound to anything? Elena snapped. This isn't my fight. This isn't my story.

The figure's laughter was low and bitter. Isn't it? You carry the blood of betrayal, Elena. You're as much a part of this as Giulia, as Alessandro. You cannot escape what you were born into.

Elena's heart pounded, but she refused to back down. Then tell me. What happened to Giulia? To Alessandro? Why is this place holding on to them?

The figure's expression darkened, her smile fading. Because betrayal has a weight that even death cannot lift. Giulia betrayed Alessandro, just as the manor betrayed her. And now it's your turn.

Elena took a step back, her mind reeling. Giulia didn't betray him. She loved him. She tried to save him.

And yet, he died, the figure said, her voice cutting. His blood is on her hands, as hers is on the manor's.

No, Elena said, shaking her head. That's not true. There's more to this.

There's always more, the figure said, her voice softening, almost tender. But the manor doesn't care for justifications. It feeds on what it takes. And now it wants you, Elena. It has chosen you to complete its story.

The glowing book on the altar pulsed brighter, its light casting eerie shadows across the chapel walls. Elena felt an almost magnetic pull toward it, as though it were calling to her.

What happens if I open it? she asked, her voice trembling.

You will see everything, the figure said. Giulia's love, her betrayal. Alessandro's death. And your place in it all.

My place? Elena repeated, her stomach twisting.

The figure stepped closer, her glowing eyes locking onto Elena's. The manor has waited for you, Elena. For generations, it has waited. Giulia's story was incomplete, her betrayal unfinished. But you… you have the power to end it.

Elcna took another step back, her heart racing. How?

The figure's smile returned, cruel and knowing. By taking her place.

The words hung in the air like a death knell. Elena's mind raced, the pieces of the puzzle finally beginning to fall into place. The manor wanted her to relive Giulia's story, to take on her pain and betrayal, to feed the cycle of suffering that had kept it alive for so long.

No, she said, her voice shaking but firm. I won't do it. I won't let this place control me.

The figure's smile faded, replaced by a cold, calculating expression. You don't have a choice, Elena. The moment you set foot in this place, your fate was sealed.

I can break it, Elena said, more to herself than to the figure. There has to be a way to break it.

The figure's laughter echoed through the chapel, chilling and hollow. You think you can defy the manor? It is older than you can imagine, its roots deeper than you can fathom. It cannot be broken.

Elena's gaze shifted to the book, the glowing light casting an almost hypnotic spell over her. She took a hesitant step forward, then another, until she was standing before the altar. Her hands trembled as she reached for the book.

Elena, the figure said, her voice low and warning. Once you open it, there is no going back.

Elena hesitated, her heart pounding in her chest. She thought of Alessandro, of Giulia, of the lives this place had claimed. She thought of the shadows, the whispers, the betrayal that had seeped into every corner of the manor.

And then, she thought of herself. Of her own life, her own choices. She refused to be a pawn in this twisted game.

She placed her hands on the cover of the book, feeling its warmth, its pulse. And then, with a deep breath, she opened it.

The light erupted from the pages, blinding and all-encompassing. The chapel disappeared, replaced by a whirlwind of memories—Giulia's memories.

She saw Alessandro, his eyes filled with defiance and love. She saw the moment he was taken, the betrayal that led to his death. And then, she saw Giulia, broken and alone, her guilt consuming her.

But there was something else. A shadow behind it all, a presence that loomed over the memories like a dark cloud. The manor itself, feeding on their pain, manipulating their lives to sustain itself.

And then, she saw something that stopped her heart.

Herself.

Standing in the manor, not as she was now, but as she had been in another life. She was smiling, holding Alessandro's hand, whispering words of love that felt achingly familiar.

Elena, the figure said, her voice distant now. Do you see? This has always been your story.

The light faded, and Elena found herself back in the chapel, the book still open before her. But now, the figure was gone, and she was alone.

Her reflection stared back at her from the polished surface of the book's cover, but it wasn't her reflection. It was Giulia's.

And then the whispers began again, louder, more insistent.

Elena… it's time.

The chapel doors burst open, and the shadows poured in, their forms twisting and writhing as they closed in around her.

Ten

The Forbidden Affair

The shadows surged into the chapel like a wave, their blackened forms twisting and writhing, filling the air with an oppressive cold that made Elena's breath freeze in her lungs. She stumbled back from the altar, the book still open and pulsing with faint light. The faint whispers that had haunted her before were now a deafening roar, a cacophony of voices all calling her name.

Elena! Elena!

The sound was unbearable, but within the chaos, a single voice rang clear—familiar, desperate. Alessandro.

Elena, hold on!

She whipped around, searching for him, but the chapel was a blur of shadows and light. She could feel the darkness pressing in, wrapping around her like icy tendrils, clawing at her resolve. The book on the altar glowed brighter, its pages turning of their own accord, each one revealing vivid, moving images as though the memories it held were alive.

Through the chaos, Elena caught glimpses of Giulia's life—moments that weren't just memories but living fragments of the past.

Giulia stood at the edge of a moonlit lake, her hand brushing against Alessandro's as they leaned close, their whispered words carried on the wind.

Giulia, Alessandro murmured, his voice soft but heavy with urgency. We can't stay here. Not like this.

She turned to him, her eyes shining with tears. Where would we go? The manor's reach... it's everywhere. They'll find us.

Not if we're careful, he said, his fingers brushing hers. You've seen what this place does to people. You've felt it. I won't let it take you.

The scene shifted violently, as though the shadows were tearing at the memory itself. Now, Giulia was inside the manor, her steps echoing through the grand hall. Her face was pale, her hands trembling as she held a piece of parchment.

I didn't have a choice, she whispered, her voice breaking. I had to protect him.

The shadows roared louder, pulling Elena back into the present. She stumbled, clutching the edge of the altar for support. The book's light dimmed, and the memories faded, leaving her alone in the suffocating darkness.

Elena! Alessandro's voice called again, and this time, it was closer.

She turned just as he appeared in the doorway, his form glowing faintly, his eyes wide with fear. You opened the book, he said, his tone a mixture of disbelief and horror.

It was the only way, she said, her voice trembling. I had to know.

You've tied yourself to the manor, Alessandro said, stepping closer. The shadows recoiled slightly at his presence but did not retreat. It won't let you go now.

The weight of his words settled over her like a heavy shroud. I saw her, Elena said, her voice barely above a whisper. I saw Giulia. She betrayed you. But why? Why would she do that if she loved you?

Alessandro's expression darkened, and he looked away. Because she believed it was the only way to save me. She thought if she gave the manor what it wanted, it would spare me.

And did it? Elena asked, though she already knew the answer.

No, he said, his voice raw. The manor doesn't spare anyone. It takes what it wants and leaves nothing behind.

The shadows surged again, and Alessandro stepped between Elena and the writhing mass. We need to get out of here, he said. Now.

But how? Elena asked, her voice shaking. The manor won't let us leave.

There's one way, Alessandro said, his gaze meeting hers. But it's dangerous. And it might not work.

I don't care, Elena said, her resolve hardening. Tell me what to do.

He hesitated for a moment, then nodded. The chapel is the only place where the manor's power is weakest. If we can sever its connection to you, to Giulia, we might be able to end this.

How? she asked.

The book, Alessandro said, nodding toward the altar. It's the key. It holds the manor's story, its power. But it also holds its weakness. If you can destroy it…

The words hung in the air, heavy with implication.

What happens if I destroy it? Elena asked.

The manor will collapse, Alessandro said. Everything it has taken will be released. Including me.

Her heart clenched at his words. But you'll be free.

Yes, he said. And so will you.

Before she could respond, the shadows lunged toward them, their shrieks filling the air. Alessandro grabbed her arm, pulling her toward the altar. We don't have much time!

Elena hesitated, her hand hovering over the glowing book. She could feel its energy, pulsing with a life of its own. Destroying it would end everything—the manor, the shadows, and Alessandro.

Elena! Alessandro shouted, his voice breaking through her hesitation. You have to do this!

With a deep breath, she grabbed the book. The moment her fingers touched it, a surge of energy shot through her, and the chapel dissolved around her.

She was back in Giulia's memory, standing in the manor's grand hall. Giulia was there, clutching Alessandro's hand as they argued in hushed tones.

I can't do this, Giulia said, tears streaming down her face. I can't lose you.

You already have, Alessandro said, his voice breaking.

The memory shattered, and Elena was thrown back into the present, the book burning hot in her hands. The shadows were closing in, and Alessandro was fighting to hold them back, his glowing form flickering like a dying flame.

Elena! he shouted, his voice desperate. Do it now!

She raised the book, her heart pounding. The shadows screamed, their forms writhing in fury. But before she could act, the altar beneath her crumbled, and the ground gave way, plunging her into darkness.

Her last thought was of Alessandro's voice, calling her name as she fell.

Eleven

Unearthing the Pendant

Elena plunged into the darkness, the cold air whipping past her as though the manor itself sought to claim her. Her hands clung desperately to the book, its searing heat a stark contrast to the numbing chill enveloping her. The descent felt endless, her screams swallowed by the void. Then, with a sudden jolt, she landed on a hard, uneven surface, pain radiating through her body.

For a moment, she lay still, her breath coming in ragged gasps. The book, still clutched in her hands, pulsed faintly, casting an eerie glow that illuminated her surroundings. She was in another chamber, its walls carved from rough stone, the ceiling so high it disappeared into shadow. The faint drip of water echoed through the space, and the air smelled of damp earth and decay.

Elena! Alessandro's voice was distant but frantic, a lifeline in the suffocating darkness.

I'm here! she called, her voice trembling as she pushed herself up, wincing at the sharp pain in her ankle.

The book's glow flickered, revealing a set of carvings etched into the stone walls. Symbols, spirals, and lines intertwined in patterns that felt both ancient and deliberate. In the center of the chamber was a pedestal, and atop it lay a small object gleaming faintly in the dim light.

The pendant.

She knew it instantly, though she had never seen it before. Its design mirrored the emblem from the letter's seal—a crescent moon cradling a rose. The sight of it sent a shiver through her, a sense of déjà vu so strong it left her breathless.

Elena, get out of there! Alessandro's voice broke through her trance, louder now, closer.

I found something, she said, limping toward the pedestal. The shadows seemed to retreat from the pendant's faint glow, their presence lingering at the edges of her awareness.

It doesn't matter, Alessandro said, appearing at the entrance of the chamber. His form was dimmer than before, his expression etched with worry. The pendant is a lure—it's part of the trap.

She hesitated, her gaze flickering between him and the object. But what if it's the key? Giulia's memories led me here for a reason. There has to be a reason.

Elena, the manor doesn't give—it only takes, Alessandro said, stepping closer. Whatever you think that pendant is, it's not worth the risk.

But something deep inside her disagreed. It wasn't just the memories guiding her; it was a feeling, an unshakable certainty that this pendant held more than Alessandro realized. Ignoring his protests, she reached out and lifted it from the pedestal.

The moment her fingers closed around it, the chamber shook violently, as if the earth itself roared in defiance. The carvings on the walls began to glow, lines of light racing through them like veins of fire. The shadows surged forward, shrieking in fury, but the pendant's glow grew brighter, holding them at bay.

Elena, what have you done? Alessandro shouted, his voice barely audible over the cacophony.

I don't know! she yelled back, clutching the pendant and the book tightly as the chamber continued to tremble.

The light from the carvings coalesced into a single beam, striking the pendant and sending a pulse of energy through the room. Elena screamed as visions flooded her mind—images of Giulia, of Alessandro, of herself in another life. She saw the night Alessandro was taken, the betrayal Giulia carried out to protect him, and the moment she realized the manor had used her love against her.

But there was more.

Elena saw the pendant being forged, its creation tied to the manor's dark origins. It wasn't just an artifact; it was a conduit, a fragment of the manor's power that had been bound into physical form. It could destroy the manor—or amplify its strength.

Elena, drop it! Alessandro's voice cut through the storm of visions, and she snapped back to the present.

She looked at him, his form flickering as the shadows closed in around him. It's a key, she said, her voice trembling. It's connected to the manor. If I can figure out how to use it—

There's no time! Alessandro shouted.

The shadows lunged, their forms twisting into monstrous shapes as they surged toward her. The pendant's light flared, forcing them back, but Elena could feel the energy draining from it, from her.

Then help me! she cried, holding the pendant out to Alessandro. If this can stop it, we have to try!

He hesitated, his expression torn. If you're wrong, it'll kill us both.

Then we die trying, she said, her voice resolute.

Alessandro stepped forward, his hand hovering over hers. As his fingers brushed against the pendant, the light intensified, enveloping them both in a blinding glow. The shadows recoiled, their shrieks filling the chamber as the energy from the pendant surged outward.

The carvings on the walls began to shift, revealing an intricate map of the manor and its hidden passages. At the center was an image of the chapel and the book, with lines of light connecting it to the pendant.

It's showing us how to end it, Elena said, her heart racing.

But before they could decipher the map, the pendant's glow faltered, and the chamber shook violently once more. The pedestal cracked, and the ground beneath them split open, revealing a dark, swirling void.

Elena, run! Alessandro shouted, pushing her toward the entrance.

No! Not without you! she yelled, grabbing his arm.

The ground gave way beneath them, and they fell together, the pendant slipping from her grasp and disappearing into the darkness below.

Elena's scream echoed through the void as they plummeted, her hand clutching Alessandro's as they descended into the unknown. The last thing she saw before the darkness consumed them was the faint glow of the pendant, pulsing like a heartbeat as it vanished into the abyss.

Twelve

The Watcher in the Shadows

Elena's descent into the void felt eternal, her body weightless and her mind awash with disjointed fragments of memory and emotion. Alessandro's hand was locked in hers, his presence the only tether to reality. The darkness around them was not merely an absence of light but a living entity, pressing against her skin, whispering secrets she couldn't understand but felt in her bones.

Then, as suddenly as they had fallen, they landed with a jarring impact. The ground was soft, almost spongy, like moss-covered earth. The air was dense and humid, carrying the sharp metallic tang of decay. For a moment, Elena couldn't move, her body trembling from the fall and the overwhelming sensation of being watched.

Elena, Alessandro's voice came from beside her, strained but steady.

She turned her head toward him, her fingers still clutching his. He was kneeling, his glowing form flickering faintly as though the fall had drained him. His dark eyes scanned their surroundings, his jaw clenched with tension.

Where are we? Elena whispered, her voice barely audible over the faint rustling that filled the air.

I don't know, Alessandro admitted, his gaze darting toward the shadows that seemed to ripple at the edges of her vision. But this... this is beneath the manor. Deeper than anything I've seen before.

Elena pushed herself to her feet, wincing at the ache in her ankle. The glowing carvings and intricate patterns she had seen in the chamber above were gone, replaced by towering, jagged columns of obsidian-like stone. They stretched endlessly upward, disappearing into a void that offered no light.

Between the columns, faint shapes moved—indistinct figures that seemed to watch from the shadows. Elena felt their gaze like a physical weight, their silent presence more terrifying than any sound.

What are they? she asked, her voice trembling.

Echoes, Alessandro said grimly. Remnants of those the manor has consumed. They're not alive, but they're not entirely gone, either.

One of the figures drifted closer, its form wavering like smoke. As it neared, Elena's breath caught—it was Giulia. Or at least, it looked like her.

Giulia? Elena whispered, taking a hesitant step forward.

The figure's face contorted, shifting between Giulia's familiar features and a hollow, skeletal visage. It opened its mouth, but no sound came, only a rush of cold air that sent shivers down Elena's spine.

Don't, Alessandro warned, stepping between her and the figure. It's not her. It's the manor's way of breaking you.

The figure recoiled, its form dissolving into the shadows. Elena wrapped her arms around herself, trying to steady her breathing. I can feel them, she said. All of them. Their pain, their fear. It's… overwhelming.

That's the manor's power, Alessandro said, his voice taut. It feeds on those emotions, weaving them into its very walls. The deeper we go, the stronger it becomes.

Elena's gaze fell to the ground where the pendant had disappeared. She knelt, brushing her fingers over the soft earth, but there was no sign of it. The loss felt like a physical wound, the one tangible hope she'd had now gone.

We need to find the pendant, she said, looking up at Alessandro. It's the only way to stop this.

He nodded, but his expression was grim. If it's here, the manor won't give it up easily.

They began to move through the labyrinth of columns, the faint rustling growing louder with each step. The air seemed to thicken, and Elena's every movement felt sluggish, as though she were wading through water. Alessandro stayed close, his presence a steadying force in the oppressive darkness.

As they walked, the shapes in the shadows grew bolder, drifting closer before retreating into the darkness. Each time, Elena felt a pang of recognition, as though she knew these faces but couldn't place them.

Why do they feel familiar? she asked.

Because they are, Alessandro said quietly. The manor pulls from your mind, your memories. It shows you what you fear, what you love, what you've lost.

Elena's throat tightened. But I didn't know Giulia's past. I didn't know any of this.

You've always known, Alessandro said, his gaze fixed ahead. Even if you couldn't remember, the manor ensured you'd feel it.

A sudden noise stopped them both—a low, guttural growl that echoed through the chamber. Alessandro stepped in front of Elena, his glowing form flaring slightly.

What was that? she whispered, gripping his arm.

The Watcher, he said, his voice low. It guards the manor's core.

Before she could respond, the growl came again, closer this time. The shadows shifted violently, and a massive figure emerged from the darkness. It was unlike anything Elena had ever seen—a hulking, twisted creature of blackened flesh and jagged bone, its eyes glowing with an unnatural light.

The Watcher.

Elena, run, Alessandro said, his voice steady but urgent.

No, she said, her voice firm despite the terror coursing through her. I'm not leaving you.

You have to, he said, glancing back at her. If it gets the pendant—if it gets you—it's over.

The creature let out a deafening roar, its massive form charging toward them. Alessandro pushed Elena behind him, his glowing form flaring brighter as he faced the Watcher.

Go! he shouted, his voice echoing through the chamber.

Elena hesitated, torn between running and staying to fight. But the Watcher's roar shook the ground beneath her, and she knew she couldn't fight it—not without the pendant.

She turned and ran, her breath coming in ragged gasps as she stumbled through the labyrinth. The shadows seemed to close in around her, the rustling growing louder, more insistent.

And then, just as she thought she couldn't go any further, she saw it—the faint glow of the pendant, half-buried in the earth ahead.

Her heart leapt as she reached for it, but before her fingers could close around it, a clawed hand shot out from the shadows, grabbing her wrist.

Elena, a voice hissed, low and guttural. *You belong to the manor now.*

She looked up, her blood running cold as she met the glowing eyes of the Watcher, its massive form looming over her.

Thirteen

The Secret Room

The Watcher's claws gripped Elena's wrist, its touch icy and unyielding. The glow from its eyes was hypnotic, burning into her own, a terrifying mix of hunger and malevolence. The pendant lay just out of reach, its faint light pulsing like a heartbeat in the shadowed soil.

Elena's mind raced, her pulse pounding in her ears. She could feel the weight of the creature's presence pressing against her chest, suffocating her with the sheer force of its being. She tried to pull away, but the Watcher's strength was insurmountable. Its grip tightened, sending jolts of pain through her arm.

You will not escape, it hissed, its voice resonating like a growl from deep within the earth. *You will feed the manor, as all who came before you.*

No, she gasped, her voice trembling but firm. I won't let you take me.

The Watcher's grip pulled her closer, its grotesque form towering over her. Its glowing eyes seemed to pierce through her very soul, exposing her fears, her doubts, and the fragile threads of hope she clung to.

Elena! Alessandro's voice rang out, desperate and defiant.

She turned her head to see him racing toward her, his glowing form flickering like a flame caught in a storm. The Watcher roared, a deafening sound that reverberated through the cavern, and threw her to the ground as it shifted its focus to Alessandro.

Elena, get the pendant! Alessandro shouted, his voice barely audible over the creature's roar.

She scrambled to her knees, her eyes locking onto the faintly glowing pendant. Her fingers brushed against the cool metal just as the Watcher lunged at Alessandro, its massive claws slicing through the air. Alessandro dodged, his movements fluid but strained.

Go! he yelled again, his glowing form flaring brighter as he threw himself at the creature, his hands igniting in a burst of light that seared the Watcher's shadowy flesh.

Elena didn't wait to see what happened next. She grabbed the pendant and bolted, her breaths coming in ragged gasps as she sprinted through the labyrinth of columns. The pendant's glow grew stronger in her hand, its warmth steady and reassuring.

The shadows writhed around her, their whispers growing louder, more desperate. They clawed at her from the edges of her vision, trying to drag her back into their grasp. She stumbled, her ankle protesting with every step, but she forced herself to keep moving.

Ahead, she saw a faint light—a doorway carved into the stone, its edges glowing with an ethereal blue hue. She pushed herself forward, her body screaming in protest, and crossed the threshold into a small, circular room.

The Secret Room

The air here was different—calm, almost reverent. The room was empty except for a single pedestal at its center, atop which sat a large, intricately carved chest. Its surface was adorned with the same crescent moon and rose emblem as the pendant.

Elena approached the chest cautiously, the pendant's glow intensifying as she neared it. She could feel the energy in the air, a pulsing rhythm that matched the beat of her own heart.

She hesitated for a moment, then placed the pendant into a circular indentation on the chest's lid. The room trembled slightly, and the chest emitted a soft hum as the lid creaked open.

Inside was a collection of objects—letters, photographs, and a small, intricately designed key. But it was the book at the center of the chest that caught her attention. Unlike the diary she had found earlier, this one was bound in black leather, its cover marked with the same glowing patterns that adorned the cavern walls.

Her fingers trembled as she reached for the book, the pendant's light dimming as it seemed to sink into the pages. When she opened it, her breath caught in her throat.

The book was alive, its pages filled with moving images and fragments of memories. She saw Alessandro standing in the manor's grand hall, his expression resolute as he faced a group of shadowed figures. She saw Giulia weeping in a hidden room, clutching a letter as the shadows loomed around her.

And then she saw herself.

She was in the same room, her face pale and determined, holding the same pendant in her hand. But this version of her was different—stronger, more certain. She turned to someone behind her, and Elena's heart stopped.

It was Alessandro.

The version of him in the book looked older, more weathered, but his gaze was the same—intense and full of love. He reached out to her, and she took his hand, their fingers intertwining.

Elena, Alessandro's voice broke through her trance, and she looked up to see him standing in the doorway. He was covered in cuts and bruises, his glowing form dim and flickering, but he was alive.

You found it, he said, his gaze falling to the book in her hands.

It's us, she said, her voice barely above a whisper. This book… it shows us.

He stepped closer, his expression unreadable. The book is the heart of the manor, he said. Everything it has taken, everything it has consumed—it's all in there. Including us.

She looked down at the pages, her fingers tracing the images. Can we stop it?

Alessandro hesitated, his gaze heavy. If you destroy the book, you destroy the manor. But you destroy everything it holds as well. Every memory, every soul.

The weight of his words settled over her like a shroud. Including you.

Yes, he said, his voice steady. Including me.

Tears stung her eyes as she met his gaze. There has to be another way.

If there is, the manor won't let us find it, Alessandro said, his tone gentle but firm.

The ground beneath them trembled, and the shadows outside the doorway began to surge forward, their forms coiling and twisting as they filled the entrance.

Elena, Alessandro said, his voice urgent. You have to decide. Now.

She clutched the book tightly, her mind racing. The pendant in her hand pulsed faintly, as though urging her toward a decision.

But before she could act, the shadows surged into the room, their force knocking her to the ground. The book flew from her hands, landing on the pedestal with a dull thud as the room was plunged into chaos.

Elena! Alessandro's voice was distant, muffled by the roar of the shadows.

And then, everything went black.

Fourteen

The Betrayal

The darkness was total, suffocating, a void so absolute that it felt as if Elena had ceased to exist. She struggled to move, to see, to breathe, but the shadows held her in their icy grip. Time lost all meaning; seconds felt like hours, and her thoughts splintered, each fragment more frantic than the last.

And then, out of the silence, came the whispers.

Elena... you can't save him. Just as she couldn't save herself.

The voice was chilling, layered with malice and truth. It sounded both alien and painfully familiar, echoing with the weight of countless betrayals.

Elena, Alessandro's voice cut through the darkness, faint but determined. Fight it. You have to fight it.

She reached out blindly, her fingers clawing through the void until they met nothing but cold air. Alessandro! she screamed, her voice cracking. Where are you?

The shadows shifted, and the whispers grew louder, forming a chorus of accusations that pierced her like knives.

She lied to you.

She used you.

You are no different.

A sudden rush of light exploded around her, and the shadows recoiled, hissing like wounded animals. Elena found herself standing in a familiar room—the grand hall of the manor. But it wasn't empty now. It was alive with movement, frozen fragments of time replaying like scenes from a shattered mirror.

Giulia stood near the staircase, her face pale and streaked with tears as she clutched a letter in her trembling hands. Across the room, Alessandro was arguing with a group of shadowed figures, his voice filled with defiance and desperation.

I won't let you take her, Alessandro shouted, his fists clenched. She's done nothing to you!

You don't understand, Giulia said, her voice barely audible. It's the only way.

Elena watched as the scene shifted, Giulia stepping forward, the letter falling from her hands. She reached for Alessandro, but he stepped back, his expression one of betrayal and heartbreak.

You knew, Alessandro said, his voice trembling. You knew what they wanted, and you still let them take me.

I had no choice! Giulia cried, her hands clasped together as if in prayer. They said they'd spare you if I—

If you gave me up, Alessandro finished, his tone bitter.

Elena's chest tightened as she watched the scene unfold, the weight of the past pressing down on her. She could feel Giulia's anguish, Alessandro's fury, the inexorable pull of the manor's dark will.

But then the room shifted again, and the focus turned to her.

Elena, a voice said softly, and she spun around to find herself face-to-face with Giulia.

But this wasn't the fragmented memory of her grandmother. This was Giulia as Elena had seen her in the book—stronger, more resolute, but with an air of sorrow that seemed to permeate her very being.

You see it now, Giulia said, her voice steady. You see what I did. What I had to do.

Elena shook her head, tears streaming down her face. You betrayed him. You loved him, and you betrayed him.

I did, Giulia admitted, her gaze unwavering. And I paid the price for it. But I didn't do it to save myself. I did it to save you.

Me? Elena whispered, her voice trembling. How could this possibly be about me?

You've always been part of this, Giulia said, stepping closer. The manor doesn't just take—it binds. It ties us together across generations, across lifetimes. My betrayal wasn't just about Alessandro. It was about you. About ensuring that you would be here, now, to finish what I couldn't.

Elena's knees buckled, and she sank to the floor, her mind reeling. I don't understand. How am I supposed to fix this? How am I supposed to undo what you did?

Giulia knelt before her, her hands resting gently on Elena's shoulders. You have a choice, Elena. A choice I never had. You can break the cycle. You can destroy the manor and free us all.

But at what cost? Elena asked, her voice barely audible.

Giulia's expression darkened, her grip tightening. The cost is everything. The manor doesn't let go easily. It will take you, just as it took me.

Elena's breath hitched as the shadows began to close in around them, their whispers growing louder, more insistent.

You can't escape.

You will betray him, just as she did.

The manor will have you.

No, Elena said, her voice firm as she stood, pulling herself away from Giulia's grasp. I won't let that happen. I won't let this place win.

Giulia's expression softened, a flicker of hope crossing her face. Then you must act quickly. The book—the pendant—they are the key. Together, they can destroy the manor, but only if you are willing to sacrifice everything.

Before Elena could respond, the shadows surged forward, and Giulia was pulled back into the darkness, her cry of warning swallowed by the void.

Elena! Alessandro's voice rang out, and she turned to see him fighting against the shadows, his glowing form flickering dangerously.

The book and the pendant lay on the ground between them, their light growing dimmer with each passing second. Elena reached for them, her fingers brushing against the cool metal of the pendant just as the shadows lunged toward her.

Elena, no! Alessandro shouted, his voice filled with desperation.

But it was too late.

The moment her fingers closed around the pendant, the room exploded with light, and the world around her shattered like glass.

She was falling again, this time into a blinding void of light and sound, her body weightless, her mind consumed by the echoes of the past.

And then, just as suddenly as it had begun, the light faded, and Elena found herself standing in the heart of the manor.

Before her stood a figure cloaked in shadow, its presence overwhelming, its voice a low, resonant whisper that sent chills down her spine.

Welcome, Elena, it said, its tone both mocking and triumphant. *The end begins now.*

Fifteen

The Masquerade Ball

Elena stood frozen, her heart pounding as the cloaked figure loomed before her. Its presence filled the room, an oppressive weight that pressed against her chest and stole the air from her lungs. Shadows coiled around it like living tendrils, and its face remained hidden, shrouded in impenetrable darkness. The pendant in her hand pulsed faintly, as though trying to warn her, but she couldn't tear her eyes away from the figure.

What do you want from me? she asked, her voice trembling.

The figure's laughter was a low, resonant sound that echoed through the vast chamber. *What do I want?* it repeated, its tone mocking. *I want what I have always wanted: to exist, to grow, to consume.*

You're the manor, Elena whispered, the realization sinking in like ice.

I am everything you've seen, it said, stepping closer, its voice carrying the weight of countless whispers. *The shadows, the whispers, the memories—they are all me. And you, Elena, are my greatest creation.*

No, she said, taking a step back, her fingers tightening around the pendant. I'm not part of you. I came here to end this.

The figure's form seemed to shift, its shadows rippling as it laughed again. *You think you can end me? This place is older than you, older than the love you cling to so desperately. You are not the first to try, and you will not be the last to fail.*

Before she could respond, the room around them began to change. The shadows receded, replaced by warm golden light. The oppressive cold gave way to a familiar warmth, and the silence was broken by the soft hum of music.

Elena blinked, her surroundings coming into focus. She was no longer in the heart of the manor but in a grand ballroom filled with elegantly dressed figures. Chandeliers hung from the ceiling, their crystals sparkling like stars, and the floor was a mosaic of intricate patterns that seemed to move underfoot.

The figures danced gracefully, their movements synchronized as though part of an elaborate performance. Their faces were obscured by ornate masks, and their laughter and chatter filled the air.

Elena.

The voice startled her, and she turned to see Alessandro standing at the edge of the crowd. He was dressed in a tailored black suit, his face half-hidden behind a simple silver mask. His dark eyes met hers, and for a moment, the chaos around her faded.

Alessandro, she said, relief flooding through her as she moved toward him. What is this place? What's happening?

It's the manor's final game, he said, his voice low. It's trying to trap you in its illusion. You can't let it.

But it feels so real, she said, looking around at the glittering ballroom. The warmth, the music, the light—it was intoxicating.

That's how it works, he said, his gaze intense. It shows you what you want, what you long for. But it's a lie, Elena. None of this is real.

She nodded, clutching the pendant tightly. Then we have to find the book. We have to finish this.

Before Alessandro could respond, a figure approached them—a tall man in a gold mask, his posture commanding. His presence seemed to draw the attention of everyone in the room, and the dancers paused, their masked faces turning toward him.

Welcome, guests, the man said, his voice rich and authoritative. Tonight, we celebrate eternity. Tonight, we honor those who remain and those who will join us.

Elena's stomach twisted as the man's gaze settled on her. You are our honored guest, he said, extending a gloved hand toward her. Will you join the dance?

No, she said, taking a step back. I'm not here to play your games.

The man chuckled, the sound sending a chill down her spine. Oh, but you've already begun. The moment you entered this place, you became part of the story. And the story must be told.

The crowd began to close in around her, their movements slow but deliberate. The air grew heavy, the warmth turning stifling.

Elena, Alessandro said, stepping in front of her, his voice urgent. You need to focus. The book is here, hidden in this illusion. You have to find it.

The man in the gold mask tilted his head, his tone almost playful. Why search for something you cannot keep? Why fight against what you cannot escape?

Ignoring him, Elena scanned the room, her eyes darting to every corner, every shadow. She could feel the book's presence, faint but distinct, like a distant echo.

There, she whispered, her gaze landing on a small pedestal at the far end of the ballroom. A black book sat atop it, its surface gleaming faintly in the golden light.

She moved toward it, but the crowd blocked her path, their masked faces turning toward her in unison. Their eyes glowed faintly beneath their masks, and their movements became jerky, unnatural.

Elena, go! Alessandro shouted, pushing through the crowd to clear a path for her.

She ran, her heart pounding as the figures reached for her, their laughter turning into distorted shrieks. The air grew colder, the golden light flickering as the illusion began to crack.

She reached the pedestal and grabbed the book, its surface cold and heavy in her hands. The room trembled, and the golden light shattered like glass, plunging her back into darkness.

Elena! Alessandro's voice came from somewhere behind her, but before she could respond, the shadows surged forward, pulling her into the void once more.

And this time, there was no light to guide her.

Sixteen

Beneath the Chapel

Elena awoke to the sound of dripping water. The air was cold and damp, heavy with the metallic tang of stone and soil. She opened her eyes slowly, her vision blurry at first, then sharpening to reveal a narrow tunnel carved from ancient rock. Dim light filtered through cracks in the ceiling, casting shadows that danced like specters on the uneven walls.

The black book rested on the ground beside her, its presence both a comfort and a reminder of the weight she carried. She reached for it, her fingers brushing its cold surface. Its pulse was faint now, but persistent, as though it waited for her next move.

Elena, Alessandro's voice came from the shadows, startling her.

She turned to see him leaning against the wall, his glowing form dimmer than before, his face etched with fatigue. He looked like a man fighting against the inevitable, yet his eyes were steady, focused on her.

You're alive, she said, her voice trembling with relief.

For now, he replied, pushing himself upright. But the manor is growing stronger. It's pulling us closer to its heart.

Elena nodded, her resolve hardening. Then we keep going. We end this.

She stood, clutching the book tightly as they began to move down the tunnel. The pendant around her neck swung gently with each step, its faint light illuminating the path ahead. The shadows seemed to recoil from its glow, but their presence lingered, pressing against the edges of her mind.

The tunnel twisted and turned, descending deeper into the earth. The air grew colder, the walls slick with moisture. Faint carvings began to appear, their patterns intricate and alien, like the language of something ancient and unknowable.

What is this place? Elena asked, her voice echoing softly in the narrow space.

The foundation of the manor, Alessandro said. This is where it began. Where it was born.

As they walked, the carvings grew more elaborate, depicting scenes of betrayal, sacrifice, and despair. Figures knelt before a towering shadow, their faces twisted in agony. Others clutched pendants like Elena's, their light extinguished as the shadow consumed them.

It's feeding on them, Elena said, her stomach twisting. It's been feeding on all of us.

Yes, Alessandro said, his tone grim. But you're different. You carry the book, the pendant. The manor fears you.

She frowned, her grip on the book tightening. If it fears me, why hasn't it stopped us?

It's trying, he said. But it's also waiting. The closer we get to the heart, the more dangerous it becomes.

They reached the end of the tunnel, where a massive stone door loomed before them. Its surface was covered in the same intricate carvings, and at its center was a circular indentation, the perfect size for the pendant.

This is it, Alessandro said, his voice heavy with both hope and dread.

Elena hesitated, her hand hovering over the pendant. What's on the other side?

The heart, he said. The source of the manor's power. If we can reach it, we might be able to destroy it.

And if we fail? she asked.

His gaze met hers, steady but filled with an unspoken sadness. Then it will consume us.

She swallowed hard, her fingers trembling as she removed the pendant from her neck and placed it into the indentation. The door groaned, ancient mechanisms grinding as it slowly slid open, revealing a cavernous chamber bathed in an eerie, pulsing light.

At the center of the chamber was a massive, glowing orb, suspended in midair by twisting tendrils of shadow. It pulsed rhythmically, like a heartbeat, its light shifting between hues of crimson and gold. The air was thick with energy, each pulse sending waves of heat and cold through the room.

That's it, Alessandro said, his voice barely audible. The heart of the manor.

Elena took a step forward, the pendant and book both glowing faintly in response. The shadows that had lingered at the edges of her vision surged forward, forming a wall between her and the orb.

Elena... The voice was low and resonant, coming from everywhere and nowhere. *You have come far, but you are not ready. The story is not finished.*

Yes, it is, she said, her voice steady despite the fear coursing through her. I'm ending it here. Now.

The shadows coiled tighter, their whispers growing louder. *You cannot destroy me. I am eternal. I am the truth of love and betrayal, the pain that binds all who enter my walls.*

You're nothing but a parasite, she said, stepping closer. Feeding on pain, twisting love into something dark and cruel. But it ends here.

The shadows lunged at her, but Alessandro stepped between her and the onslaught, his glowing form flaring brightly. Go, Elena! he shouted. I'll hold them off!

No! she cried, her heart breaking as she saw the toll it was taking on him. I'm not leaving you!

You have to, he said, his voice fierce. This is the only way. The pendant, the book—they're the key. Use them!

Tears streamed down her face as she turned toward the orb, its light pulsating faster now, as though sensing the end was near. She opened the book, its pages glowing with a blinding light that mirrored the pendant's intensity.

Elena, now! Alessandro's voice was a desperate plea, and she knew there was no time left.

With a cry, she hurled the pendant into the orb and placed the open book at its base. The room erupted with light and sound, the shadows shrieking in agony as the orb's light turned blinding.

And then, everything went silent.

When Elena opened her eyes, she was alone. The chamber was empty, the orb gone, and the book lay closed at her feet.

Alessandro? she called, her voice trembling.

There was no response.

And then, from the shadows, came a single word, spoken in a voice that was not his.

Welcome.

The shadows surged forward, and the light vanished once more.

Seventeen

The Sinister Gathering

The silence that followed the shadows' surge was absolute, pressing against Elena's ears like a tangible force. The chamber, once alive with the pulsating light of the orb, was now consumed by an unnatural darkness. Her pulse raced as she clutched the closed book at her feet, the only remaining anchor to the chaos that had unfolded moments ago.

Alessandro? she whispered into the void, her voice trembling, the sound barely carrying beyond her own ears.

Nothing. Only the oppressive quiet of the empty chamber, heavy with unseen eyes.

The shadows didn't attack but lingered, an audience waiting for her next move. She felt their collective gaze, not as physical eyes but as a weight on her soul, an unrelenting scrutiny that made her skin crawl.

Elena, the voice came again, smooth and resonant, and this time unmistakably close.

She spun around, her breath catching as the cloaked figure from before emerged from the darkness. Its form was more distinct now, its features less a void and more a pale visage that bore a chilling resemblance to her own.

You've come so far, it said, its tone almost admiring. *So close to the end.*

Where is Alessandro? she demanded, stepping back instinctively, her grip tightening on the book.

The figure tilted its head, a slow, deliberate motion. *The question isn't where, Elena. It's when. Alessandro has always been here, just as you have always been here.*

You're lying, she spat, though doubt gnawed at the edges of her mind.

Am I? The figure gestured toward the shadows, and they began to shift, their forms coalescing into shapes. One by one, the silhouettes took on the appearances of the dancers from the ballroom, their masked faces turned toward her in unison.

This is your story, Elena, the figure continued, stepping closer. *A tale of betrayal and love, of sacrifice and loss. And like all stories, it demands an ending.*

The dancers moved, their footsteps echoing unnaturally in the cavernous space. They formed a circle around her, their masks reflecting distorted images of her face.

What do you want from me? Elena asked, her voice steady despite the fear threatening to consume her.

To choose, the figure said simply.

The shadows parted, revealing two pedestals at the far end of the chamber.

On one sat the pendant, its faint glow barely illuminating the surface beneath it. On the other sat the book, its cover pulsing faintly with the rhythmic beat of a heart.

One is the key to salvation, the figure said. *The other, the key to destruction. But both will cost you everything.*

Elena's stomach twisted. Why would I believe anything you say?

The figure's lips curved into a chilling smile. *Because you already know the truth. You've seen it. Felt it. You've carried it with you since the moment you entered this place.*

She glanced at the pedestals, her heart pounding. The pendant's light was weak but steady, a reminder of its power to sever the manor's hold. The book, however, radiated a deeper, darker energy, as though it carried the weight of all the manor's secrets within its pages.

Elena.

The sound of Alessandro's voice sent a shockwave through her, and she turned to see him standing just beyond the circle of dancers. His glowing form was faint, his expression strained, but his eyes burned with determination.

Don't listen to it, he said, his voice urgent. You can stop this. Destroy the book, and the manor will fall.

No, another voice said, and Elena's heart sank as Giulia stepped from the shadows, her face ashen, her movements hesitant. The book is the only way to preserve what we've lost. Destroy it, and you destroy us all.

Elena's mind raced, her thoughts colliding in a torrent of doubt and fear. Alessandro and Giulia stood on opposite sides of the room, their gazes locked on her, their pleas tearing at her resolve.

Elena, Alessandro said again, stepping closer. The manor feeds on this—on us. It's a parasite, and it will never stop unless we end it here.

But what about the memories? Giulia countered, her voice breaking. What about the love, the lives that have been taken? If you destroy the book, you erase them. Forever.

Elena's chest ached as she looked between them. Both were right, and both were wrong. The weight of the decision was unbearable, and yet it was hers alone to make.

What happens to me? she asked, her voice barely above a whisper.

Choose the pendant, the cloaked figure said, its voice cutting through the tension. *And you may leave this place, but you will leave it empty, forgotten.*

It gestured toward the book. *Choose the book, and you may hold onto the memories, but you will be bound to them. Forever.*

The room trembled as the shadows surged forward, their whispers growing louder, more insistent. The dancers closed the circle, their movements synchronized as they began to chant in a language Elena couldn't understand.

She turned to Alessandro, her eyes pleading. Tell me what to do.

I can't, he said, his voice heavy with sorrow. This is your choice, Elena. It always has been.

The figure stepped closer, its pale face inches from hers. *The story is waiting*, it said softly. *How will it end?*

Elena's fingers tightened around the book, its warmth pulsing against her palms. She looked at the pendant, its faint glow a reminder of the freedom it promised. Her heart ached as she met Alessandro's gaze one last time.

I'm sorry, she whispered.

And then, with trembling hands, she made her choice.

The room exploded with light, and the shadows screamed as the ground beneath her feet cracked open. The dancers vanished, their forms disintegrating into ash, and the cloaked figure let out a guttural laugh that echoed through the chamber.

Elena! Alessandro's voice was the last thing she heard before the light consumed her, and the world fell away.

Eighteen

The Fractured Choice

The explosion of light was blinding, an overwhelming surge of energy that consumed Elena. She felt herself falling again, the sensation weightless and infinite, yet every fiber of her being screamed with the strain of the choice she had made. Her mind raced, replaying Alessandro's desperate plea, Giulia's anguished warning, and the cloaked figure's insidious whispers. The pendant. The book. The story.

And now, the consequences.

When the fall ended, she landed not with the jarring impact of before but with a soft, almost reverent descent. The ground beneath her was smooth and cold, the surface faintly reflective like a mirror. She blinked against the dim light that surrounded her, an ethereal glow emanating from the horizon in every direction.

She was alone.

Alessandro? she called, her voice echoing into the void.

No answer.

Her heart clenched as she looked around, the vast expanse disorienting and unnatural. It was neither a room nor a cavern but an endless space, its boundaries undefined, its atmosphere heavy with the weight of something unseen. The only constant was the faint glow from the book in her hands, its cover pulsing like a heartbeat.

Elena.

The voice came from behind her, soft yet resonant, filled with an ache that made her chest tighten. She turned slowly, her breath, catching when she saw him.

Alessandro stood a few feet away, his glowing form subdued but intact. He looked as though he'd been through a storm, his hair disheveled, his movements slower, but his eyes burned with the same intensity that had drawn her to him from the start.

You're here, she whispered, relief flooding her.

I'm here, he said, his voice tinged with sorrow.

She moved toward him, the book clutched tightly against her chest. I thought—when the light—

It's not over, Alessandro interrupted, his gaze shifting past her, toward the endless horizon. You made the choice, but the manor hasn't finished with us yet.

What do you mean? she asked, dread creeping into her voice.

Before he could answer, the ground beneath them began to shift. It wasn't an earthquake—it was something deeper, more primal, as though the space itself was responding to her decision. The reflective surface rippled like water, and the glow of the horizon intensified, casting long, shifting shadows around them.

Elena.

This voice was different. Colder. Familiar.

She turned to see the cloaked figure reemerge from the void, its presence more imposing than ever. The shadows clung to it like living armor, and its face was no longer obscured. Instead, it bore her likeness, twisted into something inhuman, with hollow eyes that burned with an unnatural light.

You made the choice, it said, its voice an eerie echo of her own. *But every story demands a reckoning.*

Elena's grip on the book tightened. I chose to end this, she said, her voice steady despite the fear coursing through her.

The figure tilted its head, a mocking smile curling its lips. *Did you? Or did you choose to preserve the story? To bind yourself to the manor's heart forever?*

Her stomach twisted. I chose to break the cycle. To destroy the pain and suffering.

Did you? the figure repeated, stepping closer. *Or did you choose to rewrite the story in your own image, just as those before you tried and failed?*

Elena, don't listen to it, Alessandro said, stepping between her and the figure. This is the manor's final attempt to trap you. It's trying to make you doubt yourself.

The figure's hollow gaze shifted to Alessandro, and it sneered. *Ah, the eternal lover. Always so certain. Always so blind. She will betray you, just as she betrayed me.*

Enough! Elena shouted, her voice reverberating through the void. I didn't come this far to be manipulated by a shadow. You're nothing but a parasite, feeding on pain and lies. I won't let you win.

The figure's smile widened, and the ground beneath them trembled violently. The space around them began to shift, fragments of memories swirling into existence—Giulia's tear-streaked face, the ballroom's masked dancers, the chapel's glowing altar. Each fragment flickered and twisted, their images bleeding into one another like oil on water.

This is your story, Elena, the figure said, its voice rising with the tremors. *Every choice you've made, every path you've taken—it all leads back to me. To this.*

No, Elena said, stepping forward, the book glowing brighter in her hands. The story isn't yours to control anymore. It's mine.

The figure laughed, the sound reverberating like thunder. *Then prove it.*

The ground split open, and a massive, swirling vortex emerged between them. The light from the book grew blinding, its energy surging in response to the vortex's pull. Elena felt herself being dragged toward it, her feet slipping against the unstable surface.

Elena! Alessandro shouted, grabbing her arm and pulling her back.

She clung to him, her breath ragged as the vortex's pull intensified. The figure loomed on the other side, its twisted form growing larger, more menacing, its hollow eyes fixed on her with an unrelenting hunger.

The story ends here, the figure said, its voice a roar. *And so do you.*

Elena's heart raced as she looked at Alessandro, his face etched with both determination and fear. She knew what she had to do, but the weight of it threatened to crush her.

Whatever happens, she said, her voice breaking, thank you for staying with me.

Elena, don't, he said, his grip on her arm tightening.

She met his gaze, tears streaming down her face. It's the only way.

Before he could stop her, she thrust the book into the vortex.

The world erupted in a blinding explosion of light and shadow, and Alessandro's voice was the last thing she heard before everything went silent.

Elena!

Nineteen

The Silent Reckoning

The explosion of light left Elena suspended in a void that was neither darkness nor brightness, but an endless expanse of nothingness. Time seemed to unravel, each second stretching into eternity as her senses flickered like a dying flame. The weight of the book's destruction still lingered in her hands, though they were empty now.

Alessandro, she whispered, her voice barely a breath.

There was no response, only an oppressive silence that pressed against her mind. She searched the void, her heart clenching as she found no sign of him, no trace of the man who had stood by her through the worst of the manor's horrors.

Then, the nothingness shifted. It began with a ripple, a faint distortion in the fabric of the void. Slowly, shapes began to emerge—walls, columns, and a ceiling that stretched infinitely high. The emptiness solidified into a vast, desolate hall, its polished floor reflecting the dim glow of an unseen light source.

Elena was no longer falling. She stood in the center of the hall, alone but for the echoes of her own breathing.

Elena, a voice called, faint and distant.

She turned sharply, her heart leaping at the sound. Alessandro!

She began to run toward the source of the voice, her footsteps echoing in the empty expanse. The floor beneath her shifted with every step, as though the manor itself were alive, rearranging its labyrinthine structure to confuse her.

Elena, the voice came again, louder now.

She skidded to a stop as the figure of Alessandro appeared ahead of her, standing at the far end of the hall. His glowing form flickered like a candle in the wind, but his presence was unmistakable. Relief flooded through her, and she rushed toward him.

You're here, she said, her voice breaking.

But as she drew closer, she saw the anguish in his expression, the tension in his posture. He didn't move to meet her, didn't hold out his hand. Instead, he stared at her as though she were a stranger.

Elena, he said, his voice heavy with sorrow. What have you done?

Her steps faltered, her heart sinking. I—I destroyed the book, she said, confusion and fear tightening her throat. I ended the manor's hold. I thought—

You didn't end it, Alessandro interrupted, his tone sharp. You released it.

Her blood ran cold. What do you mean?

He gestured to the hall around them, the endless expanse that seemed to pulse with an unnatural energy. The manor wasn't destroyed—it was unbound. Its power no longer confined, its reach no longer limited.

Elena shook her head, backing away. No. That's not possible. I destroyed its heart, its anchor.

You destroyed one piece, Alessandro said, stepping closer. But the manor is more than a single object. It's a story, a cycle, and now it's free to rewrite itself in ways we can't control.

Her mind reeled, the weight of his words crashing down on her. The hall seemed to grow darker, the shadows pressing in from every side.

No, she whispered, her voice trembling. I was supposed to stop this. I was supposed to save you.

You tried, Alessandro said, his expression softening. But the manor's story is older than either of us. It adapts, twists, survives. And now it's found its new storyteller.

Elena's breath caught. What do you mean?

The shadows surged forward, swirling around her feet like living smoke. Alessandro's glow dimmed further, his form flickering as though he were being pulled away.

Elena, it's you, he said, his voice barely audible over the roar of the encroaching shadows.

No, she said, shaking her head. I didn't choose this. I didn't—

You carry the pendant, the memories, Alessandro interrupted, his voice urgent. You are the manor's new heart.

The realization hit her like a blow. The pendant around her neck, faintly pulsing with light, felt impossibly heavy. The memories she had absorbed, the choices she had made—they had all led to this moment.

Elena, Alessandro said, his voice growing fainter as the shadows pulled him further away. You can still fight it. You can still choose how the story ends.

How? she cried, her voice raw with desperation.

He didn't answer. The shadows consumed him, and his form vanished into the darkness.

No! she screamed, running toward where he had stood. But there was nothing—only the swirling shadows and the oppressive silence that followed.

She collapsed to her knees, tears streaming down her face. The pendant glowed faintly, its light reflecting in the polished floor. The shadows began to close in around her, their whispers rising in a haunting chorus.

Tell the story, Elena.
  Write the pain.
  Become the heart.

She clenched her fists, her mind racing. She couldn't let it end like this. She couldn't let the manor win, not after everything she had endured. But Alessandro's words echoed in her mind: You can still choose how the story ends.

Summoning her courage, she stood, the pendant pulsing brighter as she gripped it tightly in her hand. The shadows recoiled slightly, their whispers faltering.

I won't let you control me, she said, her voice steady. If I'm the heart, then I decide what this story becomes.

The shadows hissed, surging forward in a final, desperate attack. But Elena stood her ground, the pendant's light growing brighter until it engulfed her completely.

As the light consumed the hall, the whispers turned to screams, and the shadows dissolved into nothingness.

And then, just as suddenly as it had begun, the light faded, leaving Elena standing in a new room.

This one was small, intimate, filled with bookshelves and a single writing desk. On the desk sat an open journal, its pages blank, a quill resting beside it.

The pendant still pulsed in her hand, its light faint but steady.

Elena, a voice whispered, and she turned to see Alessandro standing in the doorway, his form solid and whole.

But his expression was unreadable, and the room began to tremble.

You have the pen, he said, his voice low. Now write the ending.

The walls cracked, and the light in the room flickered, leaving her standing on the edge of yet another precipice.

Twenty

The Quill and the Key

Elena stared at the blank pages of the journal on the desk, her heart pounding as the weight of the moment pressed down on her. The faint glow of the pendant in her hand illuminated the desk's smooth surface, its light casting flickering shadows across the room. Alessandro stood in the doorway, his face a mask of determination and sorrow, his words lingering in the air.

You have the pen. Now write the ending.

What does that mean? she asked, her voice trembling. What ending? What am I supposed to write?

Alessandro stepped into the room, his presence filling the space with a calming warmth despite the tremors in the walls and the flickering light. The manor's power comes from its story, he said. The pain, the betrayal, the love—it's all written into its foundation. But you hold the heart now. You can rewrite it.

Elena glanced down at the journal, its empty pages seeming to pulse in time with her heartbeat. The quill beside it shimmered faintly, as if it, too, was alive, waiting for her to act.

What if I get it wrong? she asked, her voice barely above a whisper. *What if I make it worse?*

You won't, Alessandro said gently, stepping closer. *You've come this far, Elena. You've carried the memories, the choices, the pain. You've seen the truth of what this place is. That makes you the only one who can end it.*

Her fingers trembled as she reached for the quill, its surface cool and smooth. The moment she touched it, a jolt of energy shot through her, and the room around her seemed to expand. The bookshelves stretched infinitely upward, their spines filled with titles she couldn't read, and the light in the room dimmed, leaving only the journal illuminated.

Elena, a voice hissed from the shadows, and she froze.

She turned her head slowly to see the cloaked figure standing at the edge of the light, its twisted visage now fully revealed. It was her, but not her—the same features but warped, hollow, and cruel. Its eyes glowed faintly, filled with malice and triumph.

You think you can rewrite what has been built for centuries? the figure said, its voice dripping with disdain. *You think one quill and a blank page can undo the weight of this story?*

Elena clenched the quill tightly, her fear giving way to anger. *I can try,* she said.

The figure laughed, a hollow, echoing sound that made her skin crawl. *You'll fail, just as they all did. The manor doesn't end, Elena. It evolves. It adapts. You are no different from Giulia, from Alessandro, from all the others who thought they could escape.*

I'm not them, Elena said, her voice firm. I've seen the cycle, the lies, the pain. And I'm breaking it.

The figure tilted its head, a mocking smile on its lips. *Then write, little storyteller. But know this: every word you write binds you further to this place. Every choice you make will have consequences.*

The walls trembled violently, and the figure's laughter grew louder. Alessandro stepped between them, his glowing form flaring as he faced the figure.

She's stronger than you think, he said.

We'll see, the figure replied, retreating into the shadows.

Elena turned back to the journal, her mind racing. The empty pages seemed endless, each one waiting for her to shape the future of the manor. But what could she write? How could she ensure that she didn't perpetuate the cycle, that she didn't fall into the same traps as Giulia and the others before her?

Elena, Alessandro said softly, his hand resting on her shoulder. You don't have to do this alone.

She looked up at him, her eyes filled with unshed tears. What if I make the wrong choice?

You won't, he said, his voice steady. Because you care. Because you've fought for every step, every moment. Trust yourself.

She nodded, her resolve hardening as she dipped the quill into the inkwell beside the journal. The ink shimmered like liquid starlight, and the first word she wrote sent a ripple through the room, the air vibrating with unseen energy.

Once.

The light in the room flared, and the walls seemed to pull inward, the bookshelves trembling as the manor reacted to her words.

Once, there was a place that fed on pain.

The pendant around her neck pulsed brighter, its warmth spreading through her chest as she continued to write.

But pain cannot exist without hope. And in the heart of the pain, there was love.

The shadows outside the room shrieked, their forms battering against the edges of the light. The cloaked figure reappeared, its form flickering as it struggled to maintain its shape.

Stop! it roared, its voice filled with rage. You don't understand what you're doing!

Elena ignored it, her hand moving faster as the quill seemed to guide her, the words flowing as though they had been waiting for her all along.

Love cannot be consumed, and hope cannot be extinguished. The story does not belong to the manor. It belongs to those who lived it.

The walls cracked, light spilling through the fractures. The figure lunged at her, its form unraveling as it reached for the journal. Alessandro stepped in front of her, his glowing form colliding with the figure in a burst of energy that sent them both hurtling backward.

Elena, finish it! he shouted, his voice strained.

Her hand trembled as she wrote the final line, the quill digging into the page.

The manor's story ends here. The pain is over. The love remains.

The room erupted in a blinding flash of light, the shadows screaming as they were consumed. The bookshelves crumbled, the walls dissolved, and the figure's final cry echoed into nothingness.

And then, silence.

When the light faded, Elena found herself standing alone in a sunlit meadow, the journal and pendant gone. The manor was nowhere in sight.

But neither was Alessandro.

Elena, his voice came faintly, carried on the breeze.

She turned, her heart aching as she called out to him. Alessandro!

The wind carried no response, and the emptiness around her deepened, leaving her with only the echoes of his name.

Twenty-One

Whispers in the Wind

The meadow was serene, almost impossibly so, as if the chaos that had unfolded moments before had been erased from existence. The golden sunlight bathed the swaying grass in warmth, and the air carried the faint scent of wildflowers. Yet for Elena, the beauty of the scene felt like a hollow echo.

Alessandro! she called again, her voice trembling with desperation.

Her words vanished into the open expanse, swallowed by the stillness. She spun in place, her heart pounding as her eyes scanned the horizon. The pendant was gone, the journal had disappeared, and the faint connection she had always felt to Alessandro was severed, leaving a void that gnawed at her soul.

Elena...

The whisper came softly, almost indistinct, carried on the gentle breeze. She froze, her breath catching in her throat.

Alessandro? she whispered, her voice barely audible.

The whisper came again, closer this time. It wasn't a word but a faint echo of his voice, a sound that tugged at her heartstrings. She turned toward it, her pulse quickening as she followed the sound.

The meadow seemed endless, yet with each step, Elena felt a pull, an invisible thread guiding her. The sunlight grew warmer, the golden light taking on a strange, otherworldly quality that made the edges of the landscape shimmer.

As she crested a small hill, she stopped, her breath catching at the sight before her.

A solitary tree stood at the center of the meadow, its branches stretching wide as though embracing the sky. Its leaves were a deep, shimmering silver, reflecting the sunlight in a way that made them seem alive. Beneath the tree stood a figure—tall, shadowed, and unmistakable.

Alessandro, she breathed, tears welling in her eyes.

He turned to her, his face illuminated by the golden light filtering through the tree's branches. His dark eyes locked onto hers, and for a moment, the world seemed to still.

You found me, he said softly, his voice carrying a mixture of relief and sorrow.

She ran to him, her emotions a tumultuous storm as she threw her arms around him. His embrace was warm, solid, and real—everything she had feared she would never feel again.

I thought I lost you, she said, her voice breaking.

I thought I was lost, he replied, his tone heavy. But you pulled me back.

They stood there for a moment, wrapped in each other's arms, the weight of the past few days pressing on them like a leaden cloud. But as Elena pulled back to look at him, she saw the flicker of something in his eyes—a hesitation, a secret he wasn't telling her.

What is it? she asked, her heart sinking.

He hesitated, his gaze dropping to the ground before meeting hers again. The manor… it's gone, but its story isn't finished. There's still a piece of it left.

Her stomach tightened. What do you mean? I destroyed the book. I ended it.

You ended its hold on the world, Alessandro said, his voice steady but grave. But the manor's essence, its core—it still exists. It's tied to you now, Elena. You're its heart.

Her breath caught. No. That's not possible. I destroyed it to break the cycle.

You broke the cycle for others, he said, stepping closer and taking her hands in his. But the price was binding yourself to it. The manor's story didn't end—it became yours.

The words hit her like a physical blow. She pulled away from him, shaking her head. No. This isn't how it was supposed to be. I was supposed to save you, to save all of us.

You did, he said, his voice filled with quiet conviction. But this was always the cost. The pendant, the book—they were tools, but they needed someone to wield them. Someone strong enough to carry the weight of the manor's story without letting it consume them.

Her mind raced, fragments of the manor's whispers and memories swirling together in a storm of doubt and fear. What happens now? she asked, her voice trembling.

You rewrite it, Alessandro said. The manor is yours to reshape. You can turn it into something new, something that doesn't feed on pain and betrayal. But you can't leave it.

Her heart clenched at his words. I have to stay?

He nodded, his expression pained. The heart must remain in the story, Elena. It's the only way to keep it from becoming what it was.

Tears spilled down her cheeks as she looked at him. What about you? Will you stay with me?

Alessandro's silence was answer enough.

No, she said, shaking her head. You can't leave me. Not after everything we've been through.

Elena, he said softly, stepping closer and cupping her face in his hands. You gave me freedom. You gave all of us freedom. But this is your story now. It's your strength that will shape it.

Her tears fell harder, and she clung to him, her heart breaking all over again. I don't want to do this without you.

You won't be alone, he said, his voice filled with quiet conviction. The love we shared, the hope you carry—it will always be with you. That's what will make the story different this time.

The silver leaves of the tree began to shimmer more brightly, their glow intensifying as the air around them grew warmer. Alessandro's form began to fade, his outline blurring into the light.

No! Elena cried, her hands grasping at him.

He smiled, a sad but genuine expression that spoke of both love and loss. Write something beautiful, Elena. For both of us.

And then, he was gone.

The meadow dissolved around her, and she found herself standing in a room she didn't recognize, a journal and a quill resting on a desk before her. The walls were blank, waiting, the air heavy with expectation.

The pendant around her neck pulsed faintly, and a single word whispered through the silence.

Write.

Twenty-Two

The First Word

Elena stood in the center of the room, her breath catching in the charged stillness. The journal lay open on the desk, its pages pristine and untouched, yet they seemed to hum with anticipation. The quill beside it shimmered faintly, casting tiny beams of light onto the polished surface of the desk. Around her, the room was an endless expanse of white, its boundaries imperceptible, as though she floated in a void shaped by possibility.

The pendant around her neck pulsed faintly, its rhythm matching her heartbeat.

Write.

The whispered command echoed in her mind, not as a demand but as an invitation, a plea. The weight of the moment pressed on her chest, and she placed her trembling hand on the desk to steady herself. The quill seemed to call to her, its gleaming surface promising both salvation and ruin.

Elena, Alessandro's voice resonated faintly, distant but unmistakable.

She turned sharply, her eyes scanning the empty room. There was no sign of him, no trace of his presence, yet his voice lingered like a ghost, a whisper from the edges of her consciousness.

Alessandro? she called, her voice breaking.

The silence that followed was deafening.

She turned back to the desk, her fingers hovering over the quill. I don't know what to write, she whispered, her voice trembling. I don't even know where to begin.

The pendant pulsed again, its warmth spreading through her chest, and she felt an unspoken reassurance. The journal's pages fluttered slightly, though there was no wind, as though urging her to take the first step.

Taking a deep breath, she picked up the quill. The instant her fingers closed around it, the room shifted. The endless white darkened, its edges filling with shadows that writhed and whispered. Scenes began to form—fragments of the manor's history, its pain, its betrayals. She saw Giulia's tear-streaked face, Alessandro's defiance, the ballroom's masked dancers spinning endlessly in their doomed waltz.

The shadows pressed closer, their whispers growing louder.

You can't change us, one voice hissed, low and mocking.

You are part of us now, another whispered, filled with malice.

Elena, Alessandro's voice came again, cutting through the din. This time, it was closer, stronger.

She turned, her heart leaping as she saw him standing at the edge of the shadows. His glowing form was faint but steady, his dark eyes locked on hers.

You're still here, she said, relief flooding through her.

I told you, I'll always be with you, he said, his voice gentle but resolute. But you have to write the story, Elena. The only way forward is through.

She nodded, her grip on the quill tightening as she turned back to the journal. The pages seemed to ripple like water, reflecting her uncertainty, her fear.

Once, she began, the quill scratching softly against the page.

The shadows recoiled slightly, their whispers faltering as her voice filled the room.

Once, there was a place that thrived on pain, she continued, her voice growing steadier. A place that consumed love, twisted hope, and fed on betrayal.

The room trembled, the shadows swirling violently as they tried to close in. The pendant's glow intensified, pushing them back, and Alessandro stepped closer, his presence a beacon in the encroaching darkness.

But pain does not endure forever, Elena said, her words resonating with a power she hadn't known she possessed. Love endures. Hope endures. And stories... stories can change.

The journal's pages flared with light, the words she had written glowing like embers. The shadows screamed, their forms unraveling as they were pulled toward the edges of the room.

Elena! a voice roared, low and guttural.

The cloaked figure emerged from the swirling darkness, its form towering and twisted, its hollow eyes burning with rage. *You think you can rewrite the story?* it snarled. *You think one insignificant word can undo centuries of pain?*

Elena stepped back, her heart pounding, but Alessandro moved in front of her, his glowing form flaring brightly.

She can, he said, his voice unwavering. Because this story was never yours to control.

The figure lunged at them, its form shifting and contorting as it tried to break through Alessandro's light. The pendant pulsed rapidly, its warmth flooding Elena's chest, and she felt a surge of courage.

She dipped the quill into the inkwell and wrote another line, her hand steady despite the chaos around her.

The place of pain became a place of peace. The hearts it stole were freed, and the shadows faded into memory.

The journal pulsed with light, and the room trembled violently. The shadows screamed louder, their forms disintegrating as the light consumed them.

No! the figure roared, its voice echoing with desperation. *You cannot erase me!*

Elena turned to face it, her gaze steady. You were never supposed to exist.

With one final stroke of the quill, she wrote:

And the heart of the story was love, not pain.

The journal's light erupted, blinding and all-encompassing. The figure let out a final, anguished scream before it was consumed by the light, its form dissolving into nothingness.

The trembling stopped, and the room fell silent. The shadows were gone, the journal's glow fading to a soft, steady light.

Elena lowered the quill, her hands trembling as the weight of what she had done settled over her. She turned to Alessandro, her heart aching as she saw the bittersweet smile on his face.

It's done, he said softly.

Tears filled her eyes as she reached for him, but his form began to fade, the light around him growing dimmer.

No, she whispered, her voice breaking. Don't leave me.

You freed us, he said, his voice filled with both gratitude and sorrow. But this story isn't mine anymore. It's yours.

He faded completely, leaving her alone in the silent room.

The journal's final words glowed faintly, a reminder of the choice she had made.

And in the quiet that followed, a single thought echoed in her mind:

What happens next?

Twenty-Three

The Unwritten Page

Elena stood in the quiet aftermath, her hand resting on the journal. The room, now dimly lit, felt impossibly vast, its blank walls stretching endlessly in every direction. The pendant around her neck had gone cold, its light extinguished, leaving her with only the faint glow of the journal's last words: *And the heart of the story was love, not pain.*

The silence was deafening. She had expected something—a resolution, a sign that it was truly over—but the emptiness around her offered no reassurance. Her fingers trembled as she closed the journal, the soft thud of its cover breaking the stillness.

Elena.

The whisper came like a breath, soft and almost imperceptible. She froze, her pulse quickening as she turned toward the sound.

Who's there? she called, her voice echoing faintly.

The shadows began to stir at the edges of the room, curling and unfurling like smoke. They moved with purpose, converging to form a shape—vague at first, then sharpening into a figure.

Her breath caught as she recognized the silhouette.

Alessandro, she whispered, hope flaring in her chest.

But as the figure stepped into the faint light, her hope turned to dread. It wasn't Alessandro. The figure wore his face, his form, but its eyes were hollow, its expression cold.

Alessandro? she asked again, her voice trembling.

The figure smiled—a cruel, mocking twist of his lips. *Not quite,* it said, its voice carrying Alessandro's tone but lacking any of the warmth she knew.

She took a step back, her heart racing. Who are you?

The figure tilted its head, studying her with unsettling intensity. *I am what remains,* it said. *What you tried to erase but couldn't. The story may have changed, but the shadows always linger.*

No, she said, shaking her head. I ended it. The pain, the betrayal—it's gone. I wrote a new ending.

The figure laughed, a hollow, echoing sound that sent chills down her spine. *You wrote an ending, yes. But endings are fragile things, easily unraveled by those who hold the pen.*

Her gaze flicked to the journal on the desk, the weight of its presence pressing down on her. You can't rewrite what I've done, she said, her voice steady despite the fear creeping into her.

Can't I? the figure replied, stepping closer. *The story is unfinished, Elena. The last page is blank, waiting for someone to decide how it truly ends.*

Her stomach twisted as she realized the truth of its words. The journal's final page had been blank, its emptiness a glaring reminder that her work was not yet complete.

I won't let you twist it again, she said, her voice firm.

The figure's smile widened, and its form began to shift, the shadows around it rippling like water. *You don't have a choice,* it said. *The story demands balance. You removed the pain, the betrayal—but without them, what is left? Love? Hope? They cannot exist alone.*

That's not true, Elena said, clutching the journal tightly. Love and hope are enough. They have to be.

The figure laughed again, its form twisting and stretching as it loomed over her. *You still don't understand,* it said, its voice resonating with a terrible power. *The manor was never just a place. It is an idea, a force that thrives on the duality of existence. Light and dark. Love and pain. Without both, the story collapses.*

The ground beneath her feet began to tremble, and the walls of the room cracked, dark fissures spreading like veins. The shadows grew thicker, their whispers rising in a haunting chorus.

Elena, the figure said, its tone softening, almost tender. *You can't destroy me. You need me. Without the shadows, there is no light. Without the pain, there is no love. Accept this, and I will help you write the story as it was meant to be.*

She stared at it, her mind racing. Could it be right? Was her vision of a world without pain naive, destined to crumble under the weight of its own impossibility?

Elena, another voice came, faint and distant.

She turned sharply, her heart leaping as Alessandro's form appeared at the far end of the room. He was glowing faintly, his presence a beacon of warmth and light amidst the encroaching darkness.

Don't listen to it, he said, his voice steady and sure. The story is yours now. You don't need the shadows to write it.

The figure snarled, its form contorting as it turned toward Alessandro. *You,* it spat, its voice filled with venom. *Always clinging to false hope, always fighting what you cannot win.*

Alessandro stepped closer, his gaze unwavering. Hope is never false, he said. And the story doesn't belong to you anymore.

The room trembled violently, the cracks in the walls widening as the shadows and light clashed. The journal in Elena's hands began to glow, its cover burning with a heat that seeped into her skin.

Elena, you have to choose, Alessandro said, his voice urgent.

The figure laughed, its form dissolving into a swirling mass of shadows. *Yes, Elena,* it said, its voice echoing. *Choose. Will you accept the truth, or will you doom the story to collapse under the weight of your delusions?*

The pendant around her neck pulsed faintly, its light flickering as if struggling against the darkness. The journal's glow intensified, the pages turning of their own accord until they stopped at the final, blank page.

Elena, Alessandro said, his voice cutting through the chaos. Write the truth. Write what you believe.

The shadows surged forward, their whispers deafening, and the light around Alessandro flickered dangerously.

Her hands trembled as she picked up the quill, the weight of the decision pressing down on her like a physical force. The final page seemed to stare back at her, daring her to take the leap.

With a deep breath, she dipped the quill into the inkwell, the shimmering ink catching the light.

And then, with trembling hands, she began to write.

The shadows screamed, the light exploded, and the room shattered around her.

But before she could see what she had written, everything went dark.

Twenty-Four

The Forgotten Ending

The darkness was suffocating, an endless expanse where sound, light, and sensation had been swallowed whole. Elena floated in the void, her mind racing with fragments of what had just transpired. The quill had moved across the journal's final page, carving words she couldn't see but could feel, words that burned with the weight of a choice she still didn't fully understand.

Her breath came in shallow gasps, though the air felt as intangible as the space around her. She clutched at the pendant around her neck, its faint pulse a distant echo of the life she was trying to hold onto.

Then, from somewhere in the void, came a voice.

Elena.

It wasn't Alessandro's voice, nor the cold mockery of the shadow figure. It was a chorus—layers upon layers of voices, young and old, male and female, blending into a hauntingly familiar tone.

Elena, they called again, more insistent.

She turned in the darkness, though there was no direction to turn to. Who's there? she demanded, her voice trembling but defiant.

The void responded with silence.

Then the darkness shifted. It was subtle at first, a faint ripple like disturbed water, but it grew steadily stronger. Shapes began to emerge from the void—indistinct figures formed from shadow and light. They moved with a dreamlike quality, their outlines flickering as though caught between existence and oblivion.

Elena.

This time, the voice came from directly behind her. She spun around, her heart pounding, to find herself face-to-face with... herself.

It wasn't the twisted, hollow version of her she had seen before. This Elena was whole, her expression calm and unreadable, her form solid and unchanging. She wore the same pendant, and in her hand was a journal identical to the one Elena had just written in.

What is this? Elena asked, her voice barely above a whisper.

Her reflection smiled faintly, a gesture that was neither kind nor cruel. *This is the story's final question.*

I don't understand, Elena said, taking a step back.

Her reflection tilted its head, studying her with eyes that seemed to pierce through to her soul. *The story has been rewritten*, it said. *But the question remains: who will hold it?*

Elena's stomach twisted. Hold what?

The balance, the reflection replied. *The story demands a keeper. Someone to guide it, shape it, ensure it remains whole. You ended the manor's cycle, but that left a void—a void that must be filled.*

No, Elena said, shaking her head. I didn't rewrite the story to trap anyone else. I rewrote it to end the pain.

And you did, the reflection said, its tone gentle but unyielding. *But stories do not end without consequence. Love, hope, peace—they must be tended, or they wither. The story needs a heart, Elena. It needs you.*

Elena felt the weight of the words settle over her like a shroud. She had fought so hard to escape the manor's grip, to free herself and those it had consumed. Was this her fate, then? To trade one prison for another?

There has to be another way, she said, her voice breaking.

Her reflection stepped closer, the journal in its hand glowing faintly. *There is always another way,* it said. *But it comes with a cost.*

What cost?

The reflection gestured to the void around them, and the shadows began to shift again. This time, they coalesced into scenes—memories from the manor's story. Giulia's tearful goodbye to Alessandro. The masked dancers twirling endlessly in the ballroom. The Watcher stalking through the chapel's hidden chambers.

But there were new memories, too. Elena saw herself standing beneath the silver-leafed tree, Alessandro's hand in hers. She saw the journal glowing with words that shone like stars, the pendant pulsing with warmth against her chest.

And then she saw Alessandro, standing alone in the void, his face a mixture of longing and resignation.

If you take the story's heart, her reflection said, *he will be free. Truly free.*

Elena's breath hitched. And if I don't?

Her reflection's gaze darkened. *Then the void remains. The story unravels, and the balance is lost. Alessandro will linger in its fragments, a piece of the unfinished tale.*

The pendant around her neck grew heavier, its pulse quickening as though responding to her turmoil.

Elena, the chorus of voices whispered again, louder now. *Choose.*

She clenched her fists, her mind racing. Every part of her screamed against the idea of losing Alessandro, of consigning herself to the role of the story's keeper. But the alternative was unthinkable—leaving him trapped, tethered to the remnants of the manor's shattered existence.

Elena, Alessandro's voice called from the darkness, soft but steady.

She turned toward the sound and saw him standing at the edge of the void. His glowing form was faint but unmistakable, his eyes locked on hers.

I'm here, he said, his voice carrying an unspoken plea.

She took a step toward him, her heart breaking at the thought of leaving him again. Alessandro, I—

The pendant pulsed sharply, cutting her off. The journal in her reflection's hand glowed brighter, its pages turning as if in anticipation.

Elena, her reflection said, its tone calm but commanding. *It's time.*

The void trembled, the shadows swirling faster, their whispers rising into a crescendo. The final page of the journal appeared before her, glowing with a faint, golden light.

She looked at Alessandro, tears streaming down her face. I don't know what to do, she said, her voice trembling.

You do, he said, his gaze unwavering. You always have.

The journal floated toward her, its blank page waiting. The quill appeared in her hand, its surface warm and alive.

Her reflection stepped back, its form dissolving into the void as it whispered, *Write the truth.*

Elena took a deep breath, her fingers tightening around the quill. The whispers around her grew louder, the void pressing in as she lowered the quill to the page.

The first word formed, and the world erupted in light.

And then, everything fell silent.

Twenty-Five

The Eternal Echo

When the light faded, Elena found herself standing in a place that was both familiar and impossibly new. The meadow stretched endlessly around her, the golden sunlight cascading over the swaying grass. The silver-leafed tree stood at its center, its branches reaching skyward as though grasping for eternity. The air was warm, scented with wildflowers and something richer—possibility, perhaps, or the essence of hope itself.

She glanced down at her hands, the quill still clutched in her fingers. The journal floated before her, its pages filled with glowing words that shimmered like embers. The final page bore her last line, its letters shining brighter than the rest:

The story became her heart, but love gave it life.

Elena.

The voice was soft but unmistakable. She turned to see Alessandro standing beneath the silver-leafed tree, his form solid and whole, his dark eyes fixed on her with an intensity that made her breath catch.

You're here, she said, her voice trembling with relief and disbelief.

I am, he said, stepping toward her.

She met him halfway, her hands reaching for his. The moment their fingers touched, a warmth spread through her, chasing away the last remnants of the void's cold grip.

I thought I'd lost you, she whispered.

You didn't, he said, his voice steady. But we both lost pieces of ourselves along the way.

Her gaze dropped to the journal, still hovering at her side. I wrote the ending, she said. But I don't know what happens next. I don't know if I've truly fixed anything.

Alessandro smiled, a small, genuine expression that softened the sharp edges of his face. That's the thing about stories, he said. Even when you think they've ended, they go on in the hearts of those who live them.

She looked up at him, her heart aching with the weight of everything they'd endured. What happens to us?

He hesitated, his expression shadowed with a hint of sorrow. You hold the story's heart now, Elena. The balance, the light, the hope—it's all tied to you.

Her chest tightened. And you?

I'm free, he said, his voice filled with both gratitude and sadness. Free from the manor, from the pain it caused. You gave me that. But freedom means I can't stay.

No, she said, shaking her head as tears filled her eyes. No, I won't let you go. Not after everything.

He cupped her face in his hands, his touch warm and grounding. You gave me my life back, Elena. And now, it's your turn to live yours. This place, this story—it's yours to shape, to share. And I'll always be part of it, even if I'm not here.

Her tears spilled over, and she leaned into his touch, her heart breaking even as it swelled with love. I don't know if I can do this without you.

You can, he said, his voice firm. Because you're stronger than you know. And because love—real love—doesn't disappear. It echoes. Forever.

She closed her eyes, memorizing the feel of him, the sound of his voice, the warmth of his presence. When she opened them again, he was smiling, his expression filled with an unspoken promise.

I love you, Elena, he said.

I love you too, she whispered.

And then, slowly, he began to fade. His form shimmered like sunlight on water, and she reached for him, her fingers brushing his as he disappeared into the golden light.

The meadow fell silent, the only sound the soft rustling of the wind through the grass. Elena stood beneath the silver-leafed tree, her heart heavy but steady, the journal glowing softly at her side.

She looked out over the endless expanse, her mind filled with memories—of the manor, of the pain and betrayal it had held, but also of the love and hope that had endured.

The pendant around her neck pulsed faintly, its warmth a reminder of everything she had fought for. She placed her hand over it, closing her eyes as she took a deep, steadying breath.

And then, with the journal in her hands and the story's heart beating within her, she began to walk.

The meadow stretched before her, vast and full of possibility, a blank page waiting to be filled. And as she walked, she felt the echoes of Alessandro's words, his love, his hope, guiding her every step.

The story wasn't over. It never would be.

But for the first time, Elena felt ready to write it.

And so, she did.

The End.

www.ingramcontent.com/pod-product-compliance
Lightning Source LLC
LaVergne TN
LVHW011951070526
838202LV00054B/4904